Coach's Guide
To
Modern Basketball Defense

Every man who knows how to read has it in his power to magnify himself, to multiply the ways in which he exists, to make his life full, significant and interesting.

—ALDOUS HUXLEY

Coach's Guide
To
Modern Basketball
DEFENSE

by

Garland F. Pinholster

Athletic Director and
Head Basketball Coach
Oglethorpe University

prentice-hall, inc.
englewood cliffs, n. j.

PRINTED IN THE UNITED STATES OF AMERICA

13916—BC

Coach's Guide
To
Modern Basketball
DEFENSE

by

Garland F. Pinholster

**Athletic Director and
Head Basketball Coach
Oglethorpe University**

prentice-hall, inc.
englewood cliffs, n. j.

PRINTED IN THE UNITED STATES OF AMERICA

13916—BC

This book is dedicated to

Billy Carter
Roger Couch
Stephen Schmidt
Wendell Crowe
Pat Stephens Sr.

Billy and Roger were outstanding Oglethrope best defensive trophy winners. They contributed heavily to the defensive tradition at Oglethorpe. Steve, Wendell, and Pat have exhibited (in all college sports and in the game of life) a courage, a tenacity, a loyalty, and an unselfishness that epitomizes the great qualities required of the unyielding defensive performance. It seems fitting that this book of defense should carry the names of these men.

Other Books by Garland Pinholster

Encyclopedia of Basketball Drills

Illustrated Basketball Coaching Techniques

ACKNOWLEDGMENT

Production of this manuscript has been the most satisfying of my labors for Prentice-Hall, Inc. It has also been the most difficult and challenging of my three basketball books. It has been satisfying, for defense has come to be the symbol of the good fortune we have experienced in basketball here at Oglethorpe University. The task has been challenging because of the need for specifics, details in minute parts which every coach can understand. Along with this desire to present detailed, proven procedures, there has been the urge to offer more revolutionary ideas. It is my hope that the old and the new have been blended in the proper proportion.

I want to thank Pat Stephens Jr. (Head Coach, Druid Hills High School, Atlanta) for his critique of various parts of this book. His constant reminders of the high school coach's needs helped greatly. Mrs. Gregory Favre, typist, was instrumental in having the manuscript meet its deadline.

Garland F. Pinholster

Contents

PART I: THE TREND TO DEFENSE

       1. The Case for the Defense, 3
       2. Fundamentals of Defense, 17

PART II: DEFENDING MAN-FOR-MAN

       3. The Pressure Man-for-Man, 35
       4. Sinking Man-for-Man Defense, 37

PART III: ZONE DEFENSE

       5. Standard Zone Defense, 77
       6. The Matching Zone, 113
       7. Pressure Zone Defense, 121

PART IV: THE DEFENSIVE REVOLUTION

       8. Combination Defenses, 141
       9. Alternating Defenses, 165
    10. Concealed Defense, 173
    11. Rule Defense, 193
    12. Defensive Rebounding, 211
    13. Tactical Defense, 226

Coach's Guide
To
Modern Basketball Defense

PART I

The Trend to Defense

1

The Case For the Defense

A GOODLY SHARE of the credit for a good defense can be traced to the mental attitude of the team's players. Their *defensive* attitude should be *aggressive*. Too many athletes get the idea that defense is passive. Passivity creates negative actions. Aggressiveness is positive. The top defenders are all aggressive minded and aggressive acting athletes. Even while defending a goal, the players should all be inspired to think and act like attackers.

Where does the offensive attack begin? It starts on the opponent's end of the floor when ball possession is gained. The outstanding defensive basketball player really believes he can jam the ball down the throat of the man he is guarding. He believes he can "shut him out" that particular evening. He knows that the real fun of basketball—the real sense of satisfaction—is in observing the frustrations of a top scorer he has just stymied for the evening. The great defensive performer is ready to start guarding his man when he comes out of his dressing room and will guard him if he goes into the balcony and until the final whistle. He is ready to "hook up with" him, to "marry" him for that 32 or 40 minutes of action. The opponent should go home

3

with the vague feeling that a "leech" or giant octopus has attacked him. He should have nightmares dreaming about the aggressive tactics he has been made to submit to, by a wild man who wouldn't give him one minute of peace.

All our recent great teams have been good defensive clubs. California won the N.C.A.A. championship one year and went to the finals the next year. They lost in the finals the second year because their opponents played great defense even though their reputation was obtained by offense.

Many of the top teams such as West Virginia have developed great reputations for their offensive play, but they readily admit that they win many games with defense. The public wants 100 points a night and some coaches have decided to give them what they want. In the meantime, they are very careful to develop a sound defense to keep their opponents from scoring 100, too. Coach John McLendon of Tennessee A. & I. told me that their defense never received the credit it deserved. A. & I. won three straight N.A.I.A. national championships, running up big scores. The casual observer did not take note of the fact that their opponents usually scored in the sixties. When 100 points are scored, the opponent gets ball possession many times if only after a basket is scored. To hold them to a score in the sixties requires great defense. Usually, too, the team that scores 100 points fast-breaks at a great rate of speed. To return to defense at the same speed requires much more effort than it does for the team that does not fast-break.

The big basketball upsets are nearly always provided by defensive basketball teams. The great scorer left unattended will humiliate mediocre teams with mediocre talent. These same mediocre teams and players can cause some great offensive teams many moments of anguish. Check the scores of all the major upsets that occur in basketball during one season of play. You will find that nine-tenths of them are brought about by an outstanding job of individual and team defensive play.

The current basketball trend is toward defense. I will not say *back to defense* for I feel that defense was never played any better than at present. Actually, defense is almost new in scope. Never in the history of the game has defense been played as it is currently played by top teams. It has never received the attention—it has never been played individually and collectively as modern teams are playing it. Some contemporary coaches who have been active for years, such as Hank Iba and Adolph Rupp, have always played good defense. As a matter of fact, they have almost had a corner on the market because for many years no one challenged them defensively.

No team has a corner on the defensive game today; all good squads are playing it more efficiently each year. The trend is toward defense because it is absolutely necessary to spend a lot of time preparing a way to stop modern offensive formations and patterns. The bulk of attention was given to offense for so long that it developed far ahead of the defense. Scores became higher and higher. Finally, someone decided that offense had about reached its saturation point, and started devising a way to slow the offense down. Coaches were discovering something that the all-time great coaches had always known and always practiced.

The trend is to defense for it combines so well with the tried-and-true aspect of rebounding. The merits of rebounding, for some unknown reason, were recognized by the majority of coaches long before defense received its true status. The rebound is achieved primarily by good position. Good defense requires good position; therefore, it combines well with the rebound game. Rebounding and defense have one vital, common element: both require considerable courage to rise above average ability. If the coach does a good job of teaching defense, his rebound game should also be good with a minimum amount of effort. The two go together, like ham and eggs.

There was a time in the game of football when all you needed was a 6-2-2-1 defense and a 5-3-2-1 for pass defense and you were in business. The football people found out long ago that they had to be more versatile. It is not uncommon for a good football team to run 8 or 10 defenses today. Only recently have basketball people begun to realize the same thing is true in our sport.

For many years we were man-for-man or zone coaches. The man-for-man was strictly a one-on-one proposition, and if a player could not whip his man, he came out of the game. If we used the zone, it was in all probability a 2-3 or a 2-1-2 and allowed the outside shot—but no pivot play or drives. Those days are gone forever. The team that utilizes only one defense year after year must have superior personnel year after year, enough raw power to out-man their opponents. If manpower is equal or nearly so, the team that mixes its defense will have the edge over one that does not. To use the same defense all the time and actually tell your opponent what defense you will use is a tremendous aid to him. He can spend all of his offensive time working against your defense and he is therefore able to specialize in stopping your offense. At that stage you will find your offense working less effectively each year.

The basketball team that utilizes several different defenses undermines its opponents' confidence. They have worked against one type of zone and one type of man-for-man, but if you are known as a versatile defensive team, can they be really sure you won't use something entirely different? This causes them to be unsure. Lack of confidence breeds inefficiency in any physical skill.

It seems obvious that the good basketball team will need at least one type of zone and one type of man-for-man. These two can be adjusted or flexed into alternating defenses—concealed defenses with various amounts of pressure put on the offense at strategic times during the game. It is highly probable that the use of too any defenses will result in all of them being poorly executed. If this is the case, cut out everything until you can run one defense well. When it is mastered, add another one as soon as possible. It is most obvious that one defense executed confidently and strongly is better than five weak, ineffectual ones.

Defense is the greatest morale builder in the game. A strong defense gives a team a confidence—an individual and team faith that no other phase of the game can give. Rebounding effectiveness also brings about confidence (especially to the shooters), but it doesn't require the team work and sacrificial hard work that team defense requires.

Coaches lecture on team morale and its value many times during each season. If they would take the time to build a good defense they would see team pride in operation. Team defense requires everyone to pull together. This, in turn, causes a feeling of unity, a feeling of belonging that offense can never give. A spectacular shot lifts and buoys the spirits of a team especially if it is during a crucial time when two points are badly needed. A spectacular shot does not require an important ingredient—guts. Defensive play does require this quality. For this reason a great defensive play will lift a team to the heights of great and unusual effort in a way that an offensive play can never do.

We often refer to the courage required to play good defense or to rebound well. Why does it take courage to play good defense?

Try getting in a "quarter eagle" (good bent-legged defensive stance) and stay for 16 or 20 minutes. Those are average times spent on defense by high school and college players. You will find that the legs hurt, the arms ache, and that it is much more comfortable to straighten up a bit which of course eliminates the possibility of quick movement.

While we are on the subject of comfort or natural positions, let me express a theory that there is nothing comfortable or natural about good defense. The "quarter eagle" is most unnatural and tiresome. There is nothing natural about getting in front of a hard driver and getting smacked over. There is nothing natural about positioning for rebounds and getting "racked" in the kidneys by an opponent's elbows. There are many many positions in sports that are not comfortable or natural but, nevertheless, necessary. The youngster who expects to play good defense in a natural, comfortable, position will be mediocre.

However, one of the fine features of the good defensive position is its good carry-over to offense. Most athletes love offense so well that they will pay any price to help develop their offensive moves. The defensive stance with bent legs is absolutely necessary for the best execution of the jump shot, dribbling, pivoting, receiving, and offensive rebounding or tipping. Sell them on the idea that they are not just developing a position from which to play defense but one that will improve every fundamental of the game. Actually, this is quite true. I can think of no basketball skill that cannot be best performed from a bent-legged, alert stance.

There is a theory still alive in basketball that the best defense is a good offense. The idea is that you never let the opposition get set to play defense before you converge on them with the ball and a shot. If the other team employs the same theory, the game degenerates into a "basket swapping" session. It seems to me that a great deal of time and effort could be saved by allowing each team to take 100 shots unmolested from its end of the floor and declaring the winner to be the team that makes the most attempts. If neither team plays defense, there is no necessity of going through the motions. Such a game is very much like wrestling shows where the action is mostly make-believe. Such teams play make-believe defense; that is, they pretend to play so the other team will look a little better making a shot. Actually, it is easier to shoot over make-believe defenders than it would be to allow them to take unmolested shots. An unmolested shooting contest would at least put a little pressure on the shooters while make-believe defenders simply make a good shooter relax and shoot better than he normally does.

The fans should be educated by coaches, players, and press to demand half their money back when they witness such a farce. They have seen only half a game so they should pay only half price. They paid for a whole game of offense and defense, and all they have observed is the offensive half.

These observations of defense bring to mind the myth that good offensive players (especially good shooters) do not need to play defense. They are, it is assumed, valuable enough simply as offensive players. They score 40 points, and the guys they are supposed to be guarding get 30. Since their teammates are trying to run a four-man defense, each of their opponents picks an additional three or four baskets he wouldn't have gotten had the four defensive boys been allowed to play only one man instead of each one having to take care of his own man *and* the shooter's man.

For the life of me, I cannot conceive of adult, mature coaches with years of experience allowing such an illogical theory to enter into their system of play. The indefensible position of such a theory hardly warrants an attack by men. I will make only one statement to support my feeling that this system of *star* play is inefficient. Never—never have I seen a team that operated on this basis win a really important championship. They always fold in the clutch. Someone stymies their star and the four poor dumb suckers who have been carrying his lunch for him all season are left to fight their guts out for a cause destined to be lost from the first day of practice.

There is another myth about good offensive athletes who do not play defense. It is said that they are "too fragile, too finely and delicately coordinated for the offensive touch to become good defensive players. Leave the extra effort on defense to the boys who are not outstanding in other phases of the game. It is the way such boys can earn their starting role. Leave it to the boys who are not good shooters, but don't expect the hot shots to play defense, too." Good offensive basketball requires the greatest combination of talent, coordination, and split-second thinking of any sport known to man. If a player is great on offense, he must have several or all of these attributes. Defense requires good physical coordination and above average reflexes, too. It is not true that the poorly coordinated athlete can be great on defense. He can be good, he can be adequate, but not great. The truly great defensive players *must* come from among the ranks of the great offensive players. They have all the physical equipment, proven by the fact that they are outstanding on offense. They will be quick, tricky, with good hands, possess good coordination, good reflexes and other qualities of the unusual athlete. To allow them to waste these talents on one end of the floor simply because they use them on the other end is really unfair to these fine athletes. It is unfair because these players will not be able to gain the respect of their teammates, thereby cutting down on their offensive effectiveness. It is unfair to them for they will never experience the thrill of playing a full game on *both* ends of the floor. They will never gain a full appreciation for the game of basketball. They will not be able to teach a full game if they become coaches. They will actually never gain real self-respect and, what is more important in the long run, the respect or lack thereof from their team members.

A fine defense, individually and teamwise instills confidence—true confidence in a team. It is not the type of superficial, cocky confidence that the basket-swapping teams have. It is a quiet, sure feeling that they can win with the team effort required to play a good defense. They know they can rely on this phase of their game. It does not blow hot and cold. This confidence breeds upsets. It is invaluable when you face the big opponent who is supposed to beat your brains out by running and shooting. If you play good defense, you will never get beaten by the basket swappers. Great faith in defense will have a carry-over value to rebounding, shooting, and other parts of their game.

Defense is the only stable element of basketball. Every part of the game is subject to some fluctuation and variation from day to day. Passing, shooting, dribbling, ball handling, and even rebounding may see a night when the team is "on" or "off"—"hot" or "cold." The size of the playing floor, the distance of goal from wall, and other physical features may put your offense off. The only way differences in size of the playing floor can affect your defense is to help it. That is, if you normally practice on the regulation 94-by-50 playing area, the only difference in size you will see will be a smaller floor. Smaller floors will actually make your defense easier because the area you have to cover is diminished. Defense is reliable. Defense is solid —dependable—it is always there to fall back on when everything else fails. Just knowing that a team is going to perform well defensively leaves the coach free to figure ways to score more easily.

Let's develop some basketball All-Americans who receive recognition because of their outstanding defensive play. There have been All-American basketball players who played good defense, but they didn't get the All-star rating *because* of that fact. The fact that they played good defense was only incidental. The press and the fans should be conditioned to look for outstanding defensive performance. At present the athletes are about the only ones, other than some coaches, who recognize and appreciate a fine defensive performance.

Football players, baseball players, tennis players, and defensive stars of every sport except basketball get recognition. Let's change this. It's very easy.

When the press raves over your outstanding shooter, point out the fact that he earns his keep on defense, too. When your team wins a great upset victory, tell the press exactly what it was—a defensive victory. Inform them how upsets are born. Give a defensive trophy at the end of the season. Rate your players defensively. Keep defensive charts that are completely comprehensive just like you keep offensive charts. Give your outstanding defensive player the same recognition and star billing you give your outstanding offensive player. If they are one and the same, give him even more recognition than if he were one or the other. Keep defensive statistics posted in your dressing room and on the school bulletin board if possible. Cultivate your fans so that they will applaud good defensive play. Your highest praise should be saved for the lad who helps win a fine upset victory with a terrific defensive game.

In the world of politics, there is the man who is the politician's man. In the world of entertainment, there is the person who is the entertainer's entertainer. In the world of professional football, there is the unsung person who is the pro's ball player. In basketball, the player's player is always a great defensive man. The basketball player reserves his highest respect and plaudits for the gut man— the fighter—the defensive player. This fact alone would seem to encourage every basktball player to develop his defensive fundamentals and skills. Not so—far too many are willing to admire someone else as they do the hard work but get none of the credit. The world is full of people who will admire and praise the fellow who does the hard work as they wiggle in for the headlines.

Good defensive teams have a winning attitude. We have seen teams with good personnel—personnel quite adequate to win, who simply did not win because their attitude was not that of the winner. This one quality is reason enough to play defense and spend time on defense. I have never seen a good defensive team with a loser's attitude. The winning complex is a much discussed thing. We have all seen teams endure lean years as far as personnel are concerned—yet continue to win. This is because they have won so much they have the idea they are not supposed to lose. This is what we mean by the winning complex, or the winning attitude.

Defensive teams develop such an attitude quickly, for the winning attitude goes hand in hand with good morale and team pride. How can a player respect and have pride in his teammates unless he respects himself? How can a basketball player have pride or respect himself unless he plays a gut game—a game of courage—a game of defense? I will take mediocre personnel any year with a winning attitude before I will take great personnel with a loser's attitude. Beware of the lad who says, I can't do this—I can't do that. Beware of the athlete who ever says "we don't have a chance." You have plenty of opportunity to find such boys.

To find such people, purposely divide your squad so that one team is weaker than the other for a scrimmage session. There will be one cocky lad who will be with the weak team who will say, "Get ready, for we are going to whip your backsides." There will be one or two with the weak team who will say, "But, Coach, we don't have a chance." Keep the first-mentioned type. Revel in the fact that you are fortunate enough to have such a fine lad. Let him know how valuable he is. Do not loose him at any cost. Thank one and all that you have such a man—for such men are few and far between.

These are the men who win wars. These are the men

who know no such thing as the odds. They only know that there is a fight to be gloried in, and they nourish and promote that fight. They are glad to be alive and to know that there is a chance to fight. They are winners. If you have one winner on your squad—you are lucky. If you have two winners—you may win the regional championship. If you have as many as three winners—how can you lose the state championship?

During my 11 years of coaching and 22 years of playing, I have never seen more than three winners on the same ball club.

A ball team will certainly appear to have a unanimous winning attitude, a cocky spirit, but in reality it all comes from the one, two, or three lads who are winners at heart. It all comes from the very few who recognize no such thing as defeat. Such lads will win games for you when you are down 15 points with 5 minutes to play. They will tie a game up for the overtime victory when you are down 7 points with a minute to play. These lads are consistent. They are predictable. They never allow a team to lose its poise in those last few minutes. They pull a team together and cause it to relax when relaxation is needed. They fire a team up when it needs firing up. They fire the imagination and confidence of the coach. You can readily see why such men are rarely found by the dozen. They do not come along in bunches. They come along all too infrequently and the coach is fortunate who can say that he has one such man. The team with as many as three should certainly hold some sort of celebration.

Can any youngster with just average ability become an outstanding defensive player? You have heard that this is possible. I am afraid that reality will not support such a fallacious notion. Surely a youngster with average strength and average speed can become an above-average defensive athlete. The same holds true for offensive ability. An average youngster with two arms and two legs can become an above-average offensive player if he is willing to work harder than the next fellow.

To play really great defense, outstanding physical qualities are needed. That is why we say the great offensive player should also be a great defensive player.

Muscle, or its equivalent, strength, is needed. Speed is essential. Good coordination, quick reflexes, and a great deal of stamina are prime ingredients of the great defensive athlete, no matter what the sport may be. The muscle can be developed rather easily by weight lifting. Coordination can surely be improved. Reflexes can be trained to their highest potential use. Quickness is more important than sheer speed, but there is grave doubt in my mind that this element can be changed from the inherent ability one possesses. Intelligence is certainly necessary. That is, above-average intelligence. The brightest youngster diagnoses his opponent early and sets out to prevent him from making his best move. The bright youngster will talk to his opponent and use good psychology in dealing with him.

In summary, let me say that it is fatal to develop one phase of this sport to the detriment of all others. I have seen coaches go overboard on defense one year, rebounding another year, shooting still another year and yet fail to produce winners. I believe one could come nearer to developing a winner with hard work on defense—to the detriment of the other skills—for youngsters are going to practice their offensive skills on their own time. Even so, it is wise not to neglect any part of the game or any skill. We have the utmost admiration for good shooters. It takes many hours of hard work to become a good shooter. After all, the culmination of all effort in basketball is the score. If all other phases of the game are perfected but good shooting is lacking, you are not going to win. Our plea is that basketball be played on both ends of the floor. There is no place on that 94-by-50-foot playing area to rest. So many young players think that the defensive end is the rest end of the floor.

Finally, let me encourage you to develop your game on both ends of the floor so that you will not be under such a terrific handicap on that "cold" shooting night. So that our wonderful game of basketball and its complex skills will be appreciated and admired even more by the sports world. The sports world admires courageous athletes. It admires tough, aggressive play in any sport. Here is our opportunity to prove that it takes real courage to play our game. I sadly fear this is not true where good defense and good rebounding are absent. Any rabbit-brave person can play good basketball offense. Through courageous execution of rebounding and defensive skills, the basketball player can prove there is nothing effeminate about his sport. Youngsters who like football and other contact sports will become more interested in basketball if we put courage, strength, and aggressive play back into the game.

If you don't develop your defensive game, you are going to be left by the roadside as the harder working coaches strive to teach *all* phases of the game. The trend is to defense. Every good team is playing defense. The best way to prove your coaching status is on defense. If you can teach defense, if you can sell defense, if you can *produce* good defense, you can coach.

2

Fundamentals of Modern Defense

THE FUNDAMENTALS of offensive basketball can be listed by all coaches. High school players can list them. They have been enumerated and well defined for a long period of time. If coaches were asked to list the fundamentals of defense, they would all give different answers. Defensive fundamentals are rather vague and nebulous. Required skills vary from team to team and from coach to coach. Surely it is time we accepted a given list of fundamentals so that they may be defined and taught in a more precise and exact manner.

We are going to list eight defensive fundamentals. They are not necessarily the only ones and this is not necessarily the only way defensive fundamentals *could* be listed. Still, we are going to approach them in a positive manner because no accepted list of defensive fundamentals can be found. If each basketball coach begins to think about breaking defensive play down into the various fundamentals, we will certainly come up with an accepted set of fundamentals more quickly.

1. Defensive Break

Before defense can be played at all, the players must get to the defensive end of the floor in time to stop an offensive penetration. If the defensive break is lackadaisical, offensive players will penetrate the critical shooting area before an effective defensive stance or any effective defensive play can be adopted.

Defense starts as soon as you lose ball possession. The very first task is to get down court as though the house were on fire and you have to get there to put it out. After getting there, and in keeping with this same fundamental, penetration with the ball must be stopped before it reaches the critical shooting area. The man guarding the ball handler must do this job well while all other defensive players attempt to prevent their opponents from receiving in the critical shooting area.

No matter how fast a team breaks to the offensive end of the floor, its break to the defensive end should be faster. Line your players up for a 94-foot wind sprint some day and tell them afterwards that it is the speed to use while running the defensive break. The team that expends all of its energy and stamina on the offensive break will rarely have enough stamina left to get back in time for defensive play. If you are an offensive fast-break ball club, remember to run the defensive fast break, too.

2. Stance

The defensive basketball stance has been taught rather well for a number of years. The classic stance is with bent knees, wide base, staggered foot position, one arm high and one arm low. The footwork has been likened to that of the boxer since the shuffle step is used. That is, the feet slide from side to side and forward and backward without ever crossing. The eyes are glued on the midsection, belt buckle, or chest of the opponent being guarded—under the assumption that the defensive player will thus be less vulnerable to fakes.

To this classic description we will add only a few comments. We have come to call the defensive basketball stance the "quarter eagle." We use the term quarter eagle because once the stance is taught, it saves us the time of reviewing all of its features each time we discuss it. Our idea of the quarter eagle (which varies from the traditional method) is to have the higher hand as near the line of vision of the opponent as possible, and waving. We like to have the low hand cupped, with the palm facing the opponent in position to create deflections of a possible bounce pass. We want the back foot of the staggered stance to be determined by the greatest offensive threat; that is, if the opponent's most direct route to the basket is over your left foot, then that foot should be back. We operate on the theory that one can move more quickly in the direction of the back foot, since it can be moved more readily than the front foot.

The defensive player should use his offensive skill to fake with foot, head, arms, and eyes. He can fake a slap at the ball, he can fake a sag, he can fake an overplay—and in general use nearly as much deception as he would normally use on offense. Use of the arms is not exploited. A waving, moving hand is distracting to the offensive player. Most defensive players handicap themselves by not waving their front hand and blocking the offensive player's vision adequately.

3. Guarding the Man With the Ball

The man with the ball should always feel pressure, no matter how much sag or float the other team members use. Do not allow the ball handler to move about unrestrictedly any time in your front court. Some coaches refer to this as "pointing" the defense, the point always being where the ball is located.

When guarding the ball handler, the first thing to determine is whether he has dribbled or not. If he has not dribbled, and if the ball handler is not in the critical shooting area, give yourself at least a one-step cushion in which to retreat. If your man has dribbled, swarm all over him, arms waving and yelling. Talking and yelling at your opponent can prove very distracting to him. It is a most ethical and useful practice, which most defensive players fail to use.

Do *not* play directly between your man and the goal. This statement will violate most classical precepts of good defensive position. From any position on the floor, a player with the ball will have a *most direct route* to the basket. The defensive player should overplay slightly in the direction of that most direct route. If a player can dribble in only one direction, overplay slightly toward his strong hand.

During this era of the jump shot, defensive players are getting more and more in the habit of leaving their feet on fake jumps. Some coaches do not expect jump shots to be blocked and ask their players *never* to leave their feet. We have adopted the policy of having our players wait until they are *sure* the opponent's feet are off the floor before jumping. True, they will not actually block many jump shots that way. Still, they will bother and harass the shooters without the danger of leaving the feet too soon, thereby giving up two sure points via the lay-up.

3a. Guarding the Dribbler

Defending against the dribbler depends entirely on where he is located on the playing floor. If he is in the back court it is permissible to harass him but never to foul him. The professional leagues think a back court foul is so stupid that they award three shots for one. A dribbler should be picked up as soon as he enters your front court. Do not allow the dribbler to go where he wants to go. It might be a cue for their offense. If he wants to dribble into the right guard spot—make him go into the left guard position. If he wants drive into the pivot area, make him go into a corner. Herd him where you want him to go. Do not allow him to go where *he wants to go.*

Overplay his strong hand. Left handers are famous for weak dribbling with their right hands. When you get a left hander make him *prove* he can go with his right hand. Right handers usually develop a little better with the left hand, but they are still often more skilled with their "natural" hands. Why let them use their favorite? To force this issue, play about half a man on the side of the strong hand.

Don't let him drive you over screens. Anytime you are being forced backward keep your low hand behind you feeling for screens.

The quickest, easiest two points in basketball come out of what we have come to designate as the base line drive. The drive is usually started about where offensive forwards line up for a single post offense. The lay-up angle is good. The drive can be made with a minimum of one dribble. If the dribbler gets by his man, there is no one in position to pick him up. Consequently, it is necessary to practice guarding the base line as a separate and distinct part of practice against dribblers. The back foot should be the one nearest the base line. The defensive man should be on the leg of the offensive player that is nearest the base line. The defensive man should be on the leg of the offensive player that is nearest the base line.

Force the opponent to make his poorest move. Do not let him have his best move. Few high school and college players can go each way effectively. Few can drive as well as they can set. Basically, most players are drivers or setters. That is, they *prefer* to set shoot or drive for the lay-up or jump. Try to figure your opponent early. If he is a setter play him tightly and harass him all the time. If he is a driver, give yourself a little more cushion.

4. *Guarding the Man Without the Ball*

Defending against the man who doesn't have the ball is quite different from defense of the ball handler. It is the same in one important way: *the stance is the same.* Far too many players drop off and relax when their man gets rid of the ball. They are thus vulnerable to the old give and go. They are vulnerable to cuts, to fakes, to reverse pivots, and a myriad of other offensive moves if they do not stay low in the good stance we described. Rarely will you find a team of players who keeps the good stance as a five-man unit. It is one of the trademarks of good defense to see every single defensive man low whether his man has the ball or not.

The first move is to retreat when your man gets rid of the ball and keep the same stance. To retreat cuts down on the chances of the offensive give and go working on you. It lessens the hazard of cuts and break-offs of screens. It gives you a better opportunity to *feel* for screens before screens can pick you. It allows you to anticipate your opponent's next move. Once your opponent turns the ball loose, the cupped low hand should be used to feel for screens. The good defensive player will not get picked, even by a dead screen. Good team work and warning by team members helps and should occur. Do not allow your players to *depend* on that warning. They can make their own warning by using that free hand. The other hand should be up for possible deflections and to remind the defensive player to keep his eyes on his man. If possible, he *may* watch the ball out of the corner of his eye through the use of split vision, but his primary visual contact is focused on *his man.* Never, never lose sight of your man. It is the worst defensive sin a player can commit. A smart offensive player will whip you every time you take your eyes off him.

4a. Guarding the Cutter

Teams that employ pattern offenses will use more cutters than otherwise. Preparedness is nine-tenths of success in defending against such teams. The same cuts are used over and over. Such teams should have their cutters forced into routes they do not want to run. While they may be prepared for just such an eventuality, they will usually not be as strong on such secondary routes as they are on the major routes.

The greatest danger to the defender is getting rubbed off on a dead screen or a set screen that the cutters brush by. Feel for screens so that you may go *over the top* of such screens wherever possible. If the screen is too tight and the cut is well executed, go behind the screen and pick up your man as he comes off the dead set screen. You are running the risk of having him stop behind the screen for receipt of a pass and subsequent shot. Still, that is better than getting picked and watching your man go for a lay-up. If he is forced into a route he doesn't want to run in the first place all this trouble is eliminated.

Overplay the cut. If a man is cutting into the post or pivot area—beat him to his destination. If he wants to cut down the base line to a point directly under the basket— be there when he arrives and do not let him receive at that crucial point of the floor. Make him go in a direction that he doesn't want to go. Do not give the offensive player freedom of movement. Break his rhythm. Interrupt his pace and timing. Pressure him into unaccustomed moves. Make him lose his poise every time you can. An offensive player that has lost poise has lost his effectiveness.

Post cuts from the guard posts are very difficult to defend. Such cuts have been working for baskets since Dutch Dehnert and his teammates of the original Celtics started using the old pivot criss-cross. The post man with the ball is free to shoot, fake, hand-off, or delay and pass under the goal

to one of the cutters. Go over the top every time it is possible. When it is not possible, go behind the post man. Do
not switch on this play. The roll-out resulting in a little
guard on a big post man under the goal is poor percentage
play. That, of course, is better than nothing, but the very
best percentages on this play result from sliding defensive
play with the cutter keeping his man and the post man keeping his opponent.

While you are primarily responsible for one man, do not
waste yourself if he stands idly in one place and "dogs" it.
Keep your primary vision on him and co-operate with your
teammates in every way by warning of screens, helping with
the offensive post man, double teaming, and picking up
loose cutters.

While each man-for-man team will operate on the principle that there will be no loose cutters or free dribblers,
these things do happen. If so, what do you do? Do you let
them go and say, that is not my man? To pick up a free
dribbler or cutter who has eluded one of your teammates
opens you up to the possibility that your own man will
score. Surely it is better to take that chance rather than
to allow free cutters and dribblers to go in unmolested and
score on a sure lay-up. Always play the percentages. Give
a man a set before a jump. Give him a jump before a lay-
up. Give him his weakest move before his strongest move.
Use good common sense. If your man scores while you are
helping with a team member's man, the coach will understand and make allowances for that fact.

You can busy yourself with interceptions if your man
"dogs" it. Keep the arms in a state of readiness. Keep the
legs low and flexed so you can move quickly for lazy floating passes. Any floating pass belongs to any player who
can get it, offensive or defensive. Do not try for sharp,
quick passes unless they are thrown almost in your face.
By being alert while your man is out of action, you may get

an interception that is worth one and one-third points or a deflection that is worth the same amount if you deflect it to a teammate. Keep accurate statistics on interceptions and deflections. A team with a high number of deflections is usually a good defensive team. If the rate is low, you are not getting your full defensive potential.

5. *Defending Against Offensive Pivot Play*

Every team member is required to play defensive pivot— not just the post men. Versatile patterns will evolve so that each offensive man plays each offensive position. This means that the defensive men must become versatile, too. A guard cannot simply learn to defend the guard area or the forwards the forward area. Each man must be able to cope with his man no matter where he goes. One of the most trying positions to defend is the play of an offensive man in the pivotal area, the A zone area or the key hole.

A man who receives the ball in the key hole and who has the advantage of a dribble with a one-on-one situation has a great advantage. So the first step is an attempt to keep your man from receiving in this critical area. If the offensive man stations himself underneath the goal, play in front of him or face-guard him. If he plays high at the free throw line, you must play behind or on his side, according to the location of the ball. If he plays on the side of the key approximately halfway to the free throw line, get on the side that is most open for pass receiving. Never trail a cutter into the pivot area. If he is moving in that direction, beat him there so you can prevent the pass completion.

If your man does get the ball in the critical pivot area without having dribbled, make up your mind that he has the advantage but that you are not going to give him a lay-up or an unrestricted shot. First of all, you might get help. This is a good time for team members whose opponents are dogging it to help by sagging and pinching the man with the ball in that area. Do not leave your feet on a fake pumping motion. Square away on your man and crowd him slightly so that you can keep a hand in front of his vision and the basket. DON'T let him raise you up or straighten your legs for his subsequent drive. Force him to take the longer of the two shot possibilities, the jump shot. It is harder to make than a lay-up and that is precisely what he will get if you raise up. If he is foolish enough to bounce the ball once and stop, you are back on the advantage side of the ledger. Crowd and work your arms vigorously to prevent a shot at such close range.

If your man is predominantly left- or right-handed, play so that you can take advantage of this knowledge. It is possible to get a charging foul called on him.

6. Defensive Switching

It is rare in today's game of basketball that a team can be found that doesn't switch in some circumstances. Patterns, double and triple screens, dead screens, and many other offensive tricks cause defensive players to lose their man at times. If this happens and a teammate picks up his man even momentarily, these two players have performed a switch even if their coach claims they absolutely do not switch. Some teams switch only when forced to by such an emergency. Some teams switch every time two offensive players cross. Some switch when players cross where the ball is involved.

No matter what your procedure or belief, be sure your men understand it. A vague description of switching and when to use it will be a big help to the offensive team. It will cause consternation and confusion on the part of the defensive team. Uncertainty will cause them to perform their best skills poorly.

If you switch, there are two possible procedures open. Switch everytime two offensive men cross or switch on special situations spelled out by the coach. Here is one definition. SWITCH ON ALL SCISSORS ACTION BY TWO OFFENSIVE PLAYERS (OTHER THAN POST CUTS) WHERE THE BALL IS INVOLVED. Such a procedure will require many switches that are not necessary. The theory being that if switches are going to be essential in emergency situations, you might as well switch all the time to develop the habit and perfect the skill. Such a team would slide on scissors action by two or more offensive players where the ball is *not involved*. They would *slide* on *post cuts*.

Switches that lose offensive ground are detrimental. A good switch is aggressive. It will cause you to push the offense farther from the goal. It will not allow the offensive men to push closer and closer to the goal.

To switch, the two men involved *grab* each other and shove each other hard toward their new men so that there will be no doubt about the fact that the switch is occurring. The switch may be called. However, calling or switching on signal is dangerous on nights when there is great crowd noise. If your situations for switching have been well defined, calling it is not necessary.

Don't leave room for alibis in your switching system. Don't leave room for shifting of blame. Double teaming situations occur more frequently where switches are used. Be sure the defensive men know when you want them to take such a chance.

Two situations will arise where the switch is in great danger: they are the dead screen and roll-for-basket and the set shot over a stationary screen.

When the dead screen works—the defensive player was unable to feel the screen until too late, both defensive men must reconcile themselves to the fact that they are going to have to cope with a bad situation as best they can. If they give up, the offense is surely going to score. If they fight the situation hard, they might survive after all. The switch will occur when the man guarding the screener picks up the cutter or dribbler. This leaves the other defensive man to pick up an offensive man who is already *closer to the goal* than he is. He will actually be trailing him to the goal and thereby violating the old precept of never allowing your man between you and the goal. While trailing him to the goal, he can minimize the danger by raising his arms and hands high over the man's head to deflect the potential lob pass if it comes. Such a pass is quite hard to make and even harder to catch so the danger is really not as great as the position of the defensive man would seem to indicate.

The set shot over a stationary screen requires one defensive man to break around a stacked player line-up of four men, two offensive and two defensive. This danger can be lessened by simply telling the man nearest the ball to come around on the side nearest the baseline. If the other man, the stationary screener, breaks for goal the other defensive man must pick him up. If the ball handler drives opposite the direction of the defensive man who is coming around after him, the other defensive man picks him up and the aggressive defensive man must trail if the other offensive man breaks for goal.

Good aggressive switching presents basketball players with an opportunity to prove their courage. Quite often they will be charged if they stand their ground fearlessly. If they flinch or turn sideways to hook the offensive man, they will be fouling. A little head-on drill to determine just what players will step in front of a moving offensive player and those that will not is not a bad policy. Forwards get this opportunity more than any other player by switching aggressively on guard-forward exchanges.

Where switches occur, a switch-back will usually be necessary. This is necessitated by the fact that a tall forward will wind up guarding a fast little guard and vice versa. When this happens each man must determine to guard his man even at a disadvantage until there is ample opportunity to switch back. The switch-back should start with the man nearest the goal. He can tell when the danger is least and call it. He can stay with the most dangerous man—the one nearest goal—until his teammate arrives, at which time he moves outside to pick up the least dangerous of the two offensive men.

7. *Sliding*

Sliding on all criss-cross maneuvers is much simpler than switching. It also eliminates the possibility of alibis. The idea being to keep your man no matter what he does or where he goes. If he goes in the balcony, the man assigned to him goes with him and expects and gets no help from anybody with his defensive chore. Of course, it would be foolish to allow an open man to score if he should get free. Off-side sag men sould take a chance and pick up free cutters and drivers just as they would while using the switch system. Even so, sliding teams try to condition their defensive men to the idea that they shouldn't require or expect help from a teammate.

Coach Adolph Rupp—"Mr. Basketball" of all time— uses the sliding system . At the University of Kentucky, he teaches men to pick up their opponents as soon as they cross center line. Once an offensive player gets into his front court he is literally faced with a clawing wildcat for the rest of the time he remains in that area being defended by the University of Kentucky.

Of course, the secret to running a sliding defense properly is to be able to whip dead screens, criss-cross maneuvers and double screens.

On criss-cross manuevers, the man guarding the ball handler is given priority. He will go over the top of the other offensive player if possible. If that is not possible, he will slide just behind him so that he stays as close to his man as is possible.

To beat dead screens the defensive man in sliding systems must be more alert and use the hands to feel for screens. It is more necessary than ever to talk and warn each other of screens before they occur. Again, the rule is to go over the top every time it is possible. When it is not possible, the defensive man will go around the screen and pick his man up on the other side. He is thus open to a quick stop and shot behind the screen. Therefore, going behind is the least desirable of the two possibilities.

Sliding teams are able to double-team opponents on criss-cross maneuvers where the two offensive players are not in rather good scoring positions. The man who is not guarding the ball handler should initiate this move. If he feels that his man is not a threat at the moment and the entire play is some distance from the critical shooting area, it is a good time to double-team.

When executing the slide, use the hands. Use the hands on teammates to help them slide through and use your own hands to help yourself get through tight situations. Overplaying the dribbler and good execution of the other fundamentals will lessen the danger of sliding.

There are few, if any teams in the country that switch on post cuts. Teams that switch promiscuously, will slide on that particular play. So—teams that slide on all maneuvers will enjoy a little advantage on post cuts. Since they normally slide anyway, this very tough maneuver to defend will not present them with anything particularly new. Most teams slide on cuts where the ball is not involved. These teams feel they may as well slide all the time.

8. Block Out for Rebounding

The block out after a shot is listed here as a distinct defensive fundamental. In this modern day of basketball when any good high school or college player will be able to list the virtues of good position for rebounding, few of them execute this fundamental consistently. It is a fundamental skill professional teams look for in college prospects. It is a skill college coaches look for in high school prospects. It is a fundamental talked about a lot and executed well only rarely.

The block out must be performed by every defensive player—not just the man guarding the shooter. Each offensive player must find his route to the goal blockaded. Team block-out positions will make rebounding very simple. A small man may slip in for a wide rebound. Your team will get more of those *lucky* rebounds simply because no matter which side of the goal the ball comes off on you have a man here in position.

The block out can be performed in one of several ways. Some coaches teach a cross step after determing which route the offensive player is going to take. Some teach a reverse pivot from a retreat position near the goal. Our belief is that on certain cuts by an offensive player the cross step will take him out more effectively. On other offensive moves the retreat and reverse pivot will handle him better. The good basketball player should be able to use either technique to his own best advantage, according to what the offensive man does.

Once the block-out man has his body between the offensive player and the board, he should move in for the rebound using short, shuffling steps. Short, wide steps make him broader and harder to run around. Short, wide steps enable him to side step quickly if it becomes necessary to readjust his position on the offensive rebounder.

Big men must be blocked out farther from the goal. They might be blocked off and still rebound over the shoulders of smaller opponents near the goal. Small men need not be kept quite as far from the goal. The idea is simply to beat them to the goal while maintaining at least a body screen on them. The big boys, however, must be kept well away from the boards.

These fundamentals of defense should be well known to each defensive player. Some coaches will break defensive play down into fewer categories. Others will make the list longer. Playing the man without the ball and playing the cutter might be considered two separate fundamentals. Some coaches might not consider the defensive break a fundamental. Some may consider defensive faking as a separate fundamental. The most important thing is to break defensive play into fundamentals and teach them separately and distinctly the way you teach your offensive fundamentals.

PART II

Defending Man-For-Man

3

The Pressure Man-For-Man

EACH PLAYER must be conditioned to change quickly from offense to defense. This mental trick must be learned before any kind of defense can become operative. Defense is a state of mind. It can be passive, active, weak-kneed, indefinite, or masculine and aggressive. To perform offensive skills properly, an athlete must be relaxed and confident. To execute defensive skills properly, he must be the very antithesis of relaxation. He must be tense, coiled, and aggressive. He must be in a fighting frame of mind. He must be combative. This switching mentally from offense to defense requires time and experience. The difficult task is turning back to relaxed movement for offense. Most athletes can get themselves in a fighting frame of mind. In the case of football, they have no need to change that mood during the course of the game. Basketball requires the athlete to play a mental game of hop scotch if he is to reach his potential on offense and on defense. Experience and time will help the young athlete develop this ability.

Defense begins as soon as the ball is lost. The player does not wait until he gets to the other end of the floor to begin to think about defense. He begins to think defense at that very instant. Unless he has been given the task of cutting the outlet pass (to stop an opponent's fast break), his first thought is to reach the other end of the floor as fast as he can run. This run is known as the *defensive fast break*.

Some teams are known as fast-break (offensive) teams; others are considered to be slow-break teams. Every good basketball team in the nation fast-breaks. They fast break to the defensive end of the floor. This break should not be a trot or jog. It must be a full speed run. While the defensive player is executing his fast break he is looking up to spot his opponent. Some opponents are very obliging. They will always go into the pivot area or into a certain corner each time. This makes recognition very simple. Other players are not so obliging. You never know where these men will line up. That is why it is necessary to be skilled and alert at spotting quickly the number and face of an opponent. As soon as you have spotted your man, determine his relationship to the ball. Is he in position to receive and score quickly? Can you reach him in time to defend your basket? Can you help a teammate who is momentarily in trouble?

As soon as you spot your opponent, go to him and assume a defensive stance, *a defensive expression,* and a defensive attitude. Let him know by your stance, expression, and attitude that you have come to hook up with him completely and without equivocation as long as his team possesses the ball. Let him know that as far as you are concerned, your life depends on stopping him. Let him know that in order to score he is going to have to break every bone in your body.

In playing the half-court press man-for-man, your first objective is to prevent the opponent from receiving the ball. Get an arm and, if possible, part of your body between your opponent and the ball. Block his vision if possible. Body check his movement to receive every time you can. That is, stay in front of him and check his break with your body. In general, make a real nuisance of yourself even though your man has not received. You have won nine-tenths of the battle with your man if you keep him from receiving. The only thing left to do is block out when the ball goes up on the boards.

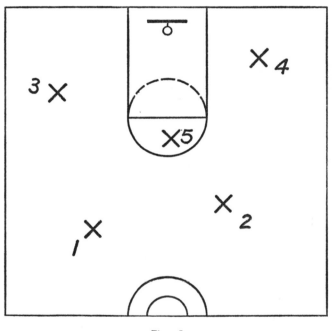

Fig. 1

This diagram will illustrate overplay. This skill is a trade mark of the more advanced defensive teams and players. The diagram shows a defensive forward overplaying a corner. True, the offensive man may break down the baseline and receive for a lay-up. The defensive man is alert for just such an emergency. He has his left arm out in front (blocking the vision) of his opponent. He has his baseline foot (right) back. He is low with the weight of his body rearward. If that offensive man cannot receive, he must come out farther to receive. If the defensive man makes his opponent receive only two steps higher than normal, he is in command of the situation. If his opponent breaks the baseline and doesn't get the ball, the offensive pattern is disrupted.

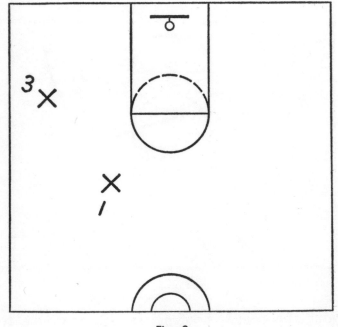

Fig. 2

This diagram offers one illustration of body checking. This offensive maneuver may be run as a set play or as part of a pattern. It is typical of the many offensive moves your defense will see a number of times during the course of a season. Note the weak side guard who is body checking his buddy's man while waiting for his own man to make his move. When his man makes his move he will pick him up and step in front of him if possible. Never miss an op-

portunity to body check. It slows up the opposition. It
frustrates them and causes loss of that all-important poise.
It disrupts timing of patterns and plays. It is also fun
when the entire team begins to take pride in *not allowing*
the opposition the freedom of movement.

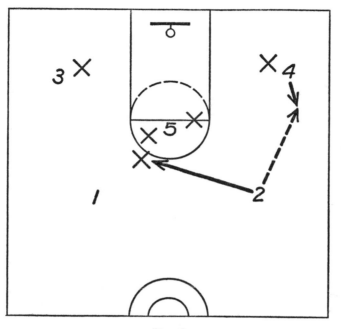

Fig. 3

If your opponent is bringing the ball down the court,
slow his progress without over committing or gambling. Do
not allow him to breeze across center line and penetrate
the critical shooting area without trouble. He is then free
to execute fakes, changes of pace, direction, etc. Slow him
up and stop him. Guide him in a direction he doesn't want
to go. Be obtuse and stubborn. If he wants to go to the
sideline, take him to the middle. If he wants to go to the
middle, take him to the sideline. Take charge of him. Don't
let him take charge of you.

If the ball handler is allowed to penetrate the critical shooting area, you no longer have a press going. Each of your four teammates is forced to "loosen" up on his man. This ground giving or "cushioning" spells disaster for the press.

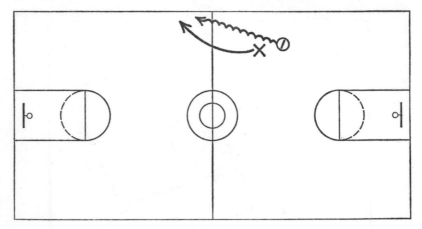

Fig. 4

Note that the defensive player picked his man up just before he reached center line. There is something about the ten-second line that makes offensive players nervous. Pick them up just before they reach that line and they hesitate enough quite often for the defensive man to take charge. This defensive player has overplayed the dribbler and forced him to a halt high and near the sideline. The offensive man is in the worst possible position to run a pattern or to pass effectively.

To play a dribbler from a standing position is quite different from picking up the dribbler who is already moving. If your man does receive (which you don't want to allow, if possible), you are still not out of the game. Get your stance and get tight enough that he cannot score over you. Then *anticipate* what his next move will be. Decide the shortest route to the goal. Block that route with an overplay. *Show* him the longest route. Overplay the danger route so that he is forced to take the least favorable of the routes to the goal. Never allow the potential driver to go where he wants to go. Make him go where you want him to go. Having given him only one choice you are left free to play that direction much more forcefully. Don't allow him to reach his destination. Slow him up, make him deviate, harass him, annoy him. Anticipate his drive. Make him get tangled up in your feet, legs, and arms with his dribble. If you can do this successfully one time early in the game, it may be enough to frustrate him for the evening.

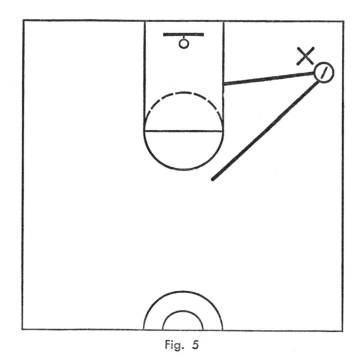

Fig. 5

This defensive man has cut off the baseline drive completely with half the width of his body. The driver is left with no driving room unless he goes toward the free throw line. It would appear to be wide open. This is not true. Since the defensive man has purposely left it open he is free to react quickly in that direction. He may force the dribbler so high that he will actually be above the head of the circle. This is not dangerous territory for a corner man. He may force the driver into a defensive post man. He may force him into a charging penalty.

When guarding a driver who has the intention of rubbing you off on a stationary screen, go *over the top* of the screen if at all possible. If you go behind the screen, the driver may stop and shoot while you are blocked by the screener. You also run the risk that he will reverse directions and catch you off balance for just such a move.

To get over the top with him, you must force him a bit higher and wider than he actually wants to go. If allowed to go directly to his destination, you will be forced behind the screener. Overplay a bit and using aggressive tactics, MAKE ROOM for your body between the dribbler and the screener.

Fig. 6

When guarding a cutter, your first aim is to prevent him from receiving the ball. If he receives at all, don't allow it to happen in the pivot area. Beat him to his destination if he runs the same route often enough for you to anticipate. By overplaying the cut you are vulnerable to a change of direction and might find your man shooting a lay-up if you don't keep your eyes on him. Your overplay has to be determined by the angle of the cut, distance of the ball from the opponent, and speed of you and your opponent. Any time it is possible, keep part of your body and one arm between your man and the ball. Body check him if you can. Be sure you don't hook or hold when body checking. However, there is nothing in the rule book which says you have to move just because an offensive player wants to pass through the spot you happen to be standing on. Here is an illustration showing

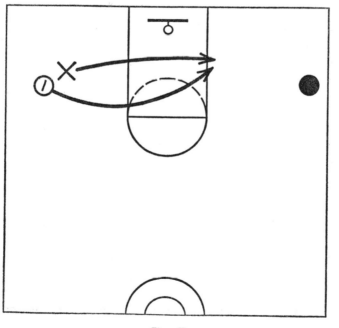

Fig. 7

how to play a cut that occurs often and is familiar during the season.

When you are guarding a cutter and he attempts to rub you off on a screen, go over the top with him if he is about to receive and behind it if there is no danger. A cutter is much more agile than a dribbler for the obvious reason that he is unencumbered with the ball. That is why we think it best to go behind screens if possible when you are guarding a cutter. Always keep your body between the ball and your man in deciding which side of a screen to pass.

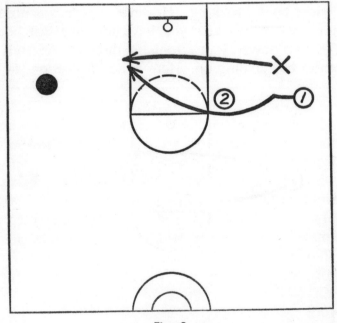

Fig. 8

The diagram just above shows the defensive man going behind a screen because it is the most direct route for interception of the cutter. The diagram (See Fig. 9) shows the defensive man going over the top because he can keep his body between the man and the ball.

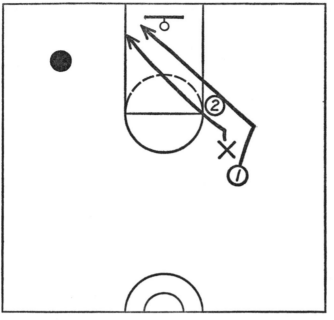

Fig. 9

To defend the post area well, each team member should be drilled the same way. If no one but your center or post man practices guarding in the post area, he is the only one that will be able to defend well in that spot. Normally, he should be the most skilled defensive post man but not the only one. Since every defensive man will end up play-ing a man in the pivotal area at one time or another, each man should drill in that position.

Again, the first objective is to prevent your opponent from receiving in that area. If an offensive man receives in a 15-foot radius of the basket, with his back to the goal, not having dribbled, with many fakes at his disposal, he definitely has an advantage over the defense. If he does receive in that area get your legs bent and your arms high. The arms should be higher than normal and closer than normal to the offensive player's vision. Do not allow the opponent to *raise you up*. Be sure to keep the legs bent.

If you straighten up, he has only a one step drive for lay-up. Fix your vision on his belt and work your arms more than usual. He already has you at a disadvantage; don't enhance that advantage by straightening up. It is far better for him to shoot a short jump shot than a short lay-up.

Faking is not a weapon totally reserved for the offensive players. It can be employed to great advantage by the defensive man. Fake at the ball. Fake at his face with your hand. Fake to intercept his pass. Fake to let him by, then body check. Fake to body check, step back, then body check. It is a weapon employed all too rarely by defensive men. Some defensive men simply assume faking is for the sole use of the man in possession of the ball.

Some athletes are naturally "pepper pot" type individuals. These individuals should be encouraged to exploit this trait to fullest advantage while playing defensive basketball. The silent type must be encouraged to talk enough to warn of screens, call switches, etc. Some offensive players are easily frustrated by a talking guard. There seems to be little doubt that many contests in all sports have been decided by talking. Some athletes can talk you out of a game. Talk to your opponent about the weather, his girl friend, his region or state, anything to get his mind off basketball. Anything, of course, that is not profane or bigoted. Anything that would fall in the realm of poor sportsmanship might inspire the opponent to greater effort.

Talking serves another purpose. It stimulates your teammates. It lifts them to greater efforts. It discourages the opposition and detracts from any signals they might be trying to use. It is good to call signals with them, if they are the type of team that uses verbal signals for any purpose. For instance, some teams call numbers for an out-of-bounds play. Every one of your men should give a signal, too. It might prevent them from getting their own signal and might possibly cause them some disunity.

To use pressure man-for-man effectively, every chance to double-team the opposition should be utilized. The double team should take place when two offensive players cross, involving the ball on a lateral criss-cross maneuver. The ball is far enough from the basket that no immediate threat is great. A double team can be attempted and the defense will still be able to recoup if they miss on the double team.

Double team with the use of the post man when cutters move by for hand-off passes. The post man may step in front of the receiver and the defensive man already on the receiver will form a very difficult situation for the offensive man. The corner of the floor of any half court is a good place to double team. The sidelines provide a third and even a fourth man for aid in the double team effort.

Fig. 10

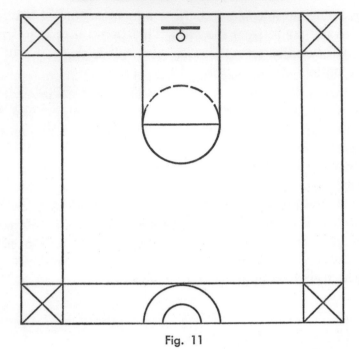

Fig. 11

The diagram (See Fig. 10) shows a double team situation with two offensive men crossing in front of the goal and moving laterally. The diagram (See Fig. 12) shows the places on the floor that are especially conducive to effective double teaming. The "X" marks in the corner indicate that these are the best places on the floor to harass the opposition. Once the double team is initiated, the two defensive men should move in tight and get their own feet as close to each other as possible forming a pen for the offensive player to escape. They should wave their arms vigorously and continuously in windmill fashion. The ball handler should be forced to throw the ball *high* if at all. Each of the other three defensive players should be especially alert for the interception. They should anticipate the place or places where the ball handler may pass the ball. Every passing opportunity should be cut off from the man being double teamed. The two men double teaming should not try to steal the ball. Their main task is to force the ball handler into throwing the ball high so it can be intercepted.

Full court pressure is exerted using the same principles that are used for half court pressure. The greatest difference lies in the fact that the offense is met with pressure long before it gets to center line. There also should be more overplay of each individual who is a potential receiver.

The defensive guards can double team the guard who is in bounds and ready to receive. They can play their men normally and attempt to get the double team situation later while putting a great deal of pressure on the passer trying to get the ball in bounds.

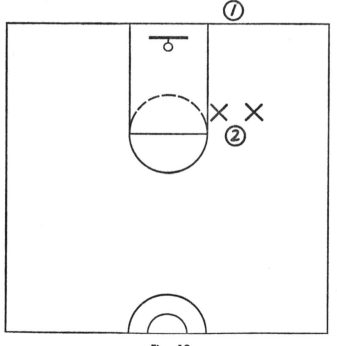

Fig. 12

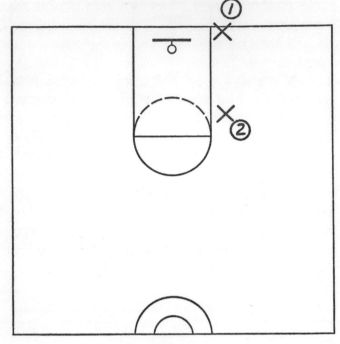

Fig. 13

Each defensive player up court should attempt to play in such a position that they could intercept a long pass. More gambling may be permitted in the back court since the defensive man has almost 94 feet in which to recover to a more advantageous spot if he over-commits.

Pendulum Pressure

This pressure defense is used on a half court basis. It works most effectively against pattern teams. It requires a strenuous overplay of the two nearest men to the ball. This overplay creates a *gap* into which the ball handler is forced. When he enters the gap he is momentarily double teamed while all other offensive players are harassed as much as possible.

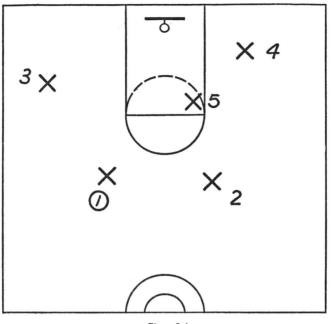

Fig. 14

Note the obvious driving room down the middle for the left guard. When he starts his drive, it is cut off by the defensive right guard. The defensive forwards immediately apply pressure by use of the overplay. The defensive post man makes every effort to prevent his man from receiving. If any of these men receive, the pendulum of overplay must swing so that the two nearest potential receivers are shut off completely. The nearest defensive man will stop the driver when he starts through the gap thus created.

If the offensive right guard breaks, the defensive right guard will go with him after stopping the dribbler. Fig. 16 —on page 52—shows how the pendulum would swing if the defensive right guard should allow his man to receive.

Fig. 17 is a pendulum swing if the offensive forward should receive. Note that the defensive left guard must be

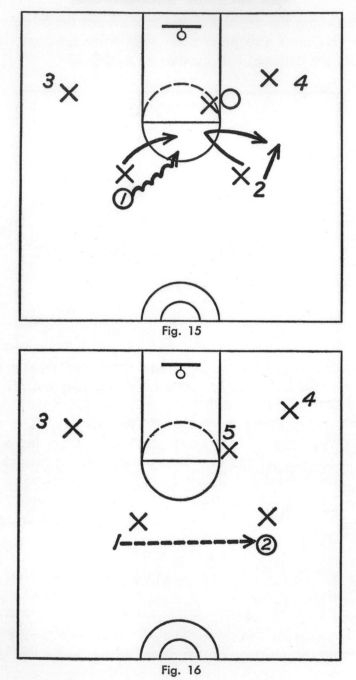

Fig. 15

Fig. 16

alert to stop the dribbler if he starts toward the free throw line. He must also prevent his man from receiving, thus giving the harassed ball handler an outlet.

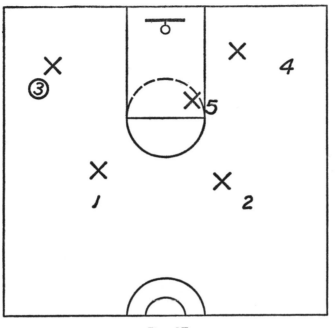

Fig. 17

The overplay on the other side of the floor would be the same as that shown here for the left side. Every effort should be made to prevent a penetration of the ball to the post man. If the pivot man does receive, each defensive player should drop off to a normal position until the ball goes back to one of the periphery men. Then the pendulum action can be initiated again (See Fig. 18).

When a defensive assignment is made, the coach should appeal strongly to the individual's pride. For instance, Jimmy Jones is assigned to guard John Smith. Jimmy's job is to thwart John from scoring. If he can do this successfully, he remains in the game. If he cannot, he does

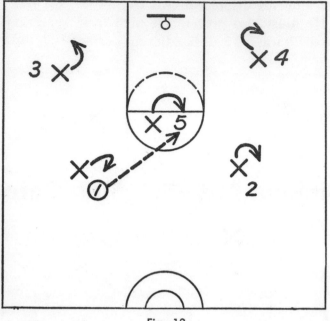

Fig. 18

not remain in the game. He should not expect to remain in the game. Pressure man-for-man is as simple as that. You can whip your man or he can whip you. Any athlete who is really *athletic* by nature, upbringing, and attitude will have enough *pride* to fight his heart out under such circumstances, with this challenge ringing in his ears. If a boy does not have this pride he is wasting his time in the combative world of athletics.

4

Sinking Man-For-Man Defense

S INKING MAN-FOR-MAN DEFENSE was made famous by
Coach Hank Iba from Oklahoma State. Used properly, it
becomes a strenuous, hardworking, multi-purpose defense.
Used improperly, as is so often the case, sagging defense
practices result in little more than a rest period for four
men while one man gives token effort and attention to the
ball handler.

The very first task is to sell team members on the idea
that when they sink or sag it is not to be a rest period. It
is to be considered a strenuous, arm-waving, coordinated,
cooperative effort by all five members. This effort should
produce numerous deflections and a terrific psychological
barrier to the offense. At its best the sinking man-for-man
appears to be almost impenetrable. It appears to be a
solid knot of arm-waving maniacs who will not allow a
decent shot to be taken in the critical shooting area.

The sinking man-for-man is sometimes employed so
effectively that the offense cannot determine the precise
nature of the defense. Because of the sag and because of
the arm-waving, the offense might well be led into thinking
they are attacking a zone defense or a combination defense

of some sort. This is especially true if the sinking man-for-man team uses switching tactics and does not call the switches so that the offense can hear them. Sinking man-for-man is related to zone in other ways. It virtually eliminates pivot play. The offensive post man finds himself surrounded by four men while one of the defensive players harasses the ball handler. He finds it difficult to receive and even more difficult to do anything with the ball. Middle lane drives are eliminated. As a matter of fact, there is little ball movement as a result of passing or dribbling other than around the periphery or outside edges of the defense.

Fig. 19

Sinking man-for-man defense creates ideal rebounding conditions. The defensive men are already nearer the goal than the offensive men. In this case, the sinking players are almost shoulder to shoulder and foot to foot when the ball hits the backboards. They present a solid human wall blocking out offensive players from the boards. The only real rebounding danger is that the block off will be executed too close to the goal so that wide rebounds are received by the offense.

Arm movement is of utmost importance to a good sinking man-for-man. Without arm movement by all five men, cross-court passes may be made that would take advantage of the off-side sag. Some offenses treat an attack of sinking man-for-man as though it were a zone. This means they move the ball around the periphery for a jump shot on the weak side. The sag could be hurt in this manner without good arm movement.

The most important single facet of sinking man-for-man defense is good harassment of the ball handler. Many coaches call this pointing the ball. The basic idea is to have all players cue their position by the position of the ball and its relationship with the goal. The player guarding the man who has possession will move in close to prevent the shot.

Basically, there are only two ways to defend against the ball handler in the front court. You can defend against the drive or defend against the shot. Some players are great *drivers* and poor shots. In this event it might be appropriate to defend primarily against the *dribble* threat. This would require the defensive player to back off. It is our belief that many high school and college players can shoot the jump shot so quickly and accurately that we must give our primary attention to the *shot*. Therefore it is necessary for the man guarding the ball to move in close enough for arm movement to block the vision of the shooter. He should take his position in such a manner that the most dangerous driving route is cut off or overplayed. He is close enough to prevent a shot. The only real good alternative for the ball handler is a pass or dribble in the direction that is *shown* him. Let's take a look at one sinking man-for-man situation and see where each man plays and why.

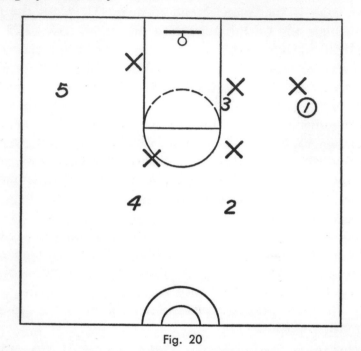

Fig. 20

The first defensive man is guarding the man with the ball—right forward. He is overplaying the base line to prevent a dribble or drive in that direction. To do this properly, his left foot will be back and his right arm will be blocking the vision of the ball handler. The ball handler may drive toward the key hole or pass to his team-mate—the right guard. As long as the right forward has the ball and is contained by the defensive player assigned to him, all the other defensive men will maintain the sag positions shown here. They should have both arms up with the major part of their vision focused on their own man and observe the ball handler using peripheral vision. Men 2X and 3X have the least sag of the remaining defensive players. They are guarding men adjacent to the ball and are therefore in the greater danger. Player 2X has sagged enough to pinch the ball handler's driving route to the key hole or recover quickly to a tight position on his own man if that man should receive. 3X plays the post man high and on the outside to prevent a pass. His first thought always is to prevent his man from receiving. Player 4X will play as deep as the foul line depending on his speed. Two passes will be required for his man to receive the ball. He should gauge how far he could move during the interval of time required to make two passes. Number 5X has the deepest sag of any man. In order for his man to receive, three passes would have to be executed unless a high, floating pass was thrown laterally across the court. If a cross-court pass is used and all five defensive men have their arms high for deflecting purposes, 5X can reach his man in plenty of time and possibly intercept.

Note that the middle is jammed. The base line drive is stymied. The outside shot is stopped. The greatest threat here is peripheral passing—quick movement of the ball to take advantage of slow recovery by weak side defensive men. Quick movement of the ball may take advantage of lazy defensive players who think the sinking man-for-man is a resting defense. We can see why some teams attack this defense just as though it were a zone. Actually, the defensive players should use good zone arm movement principles along with the best man-for-man foot work principles. Here are some other ball positions showing the sag position of all five men (Fig. 21).

The right guard has received the ball: 2X overplays the middle drive; 1X drops off to a quick recovery position; 3X moves high on the inside of his man; 4X moves out to the head of the circle and in one step to pinch the middle in the event a middle drive is attempted. Number 5X moves to a position where he may pick up his man tightly, in time, if two quick passes should be made (Fig. 22).

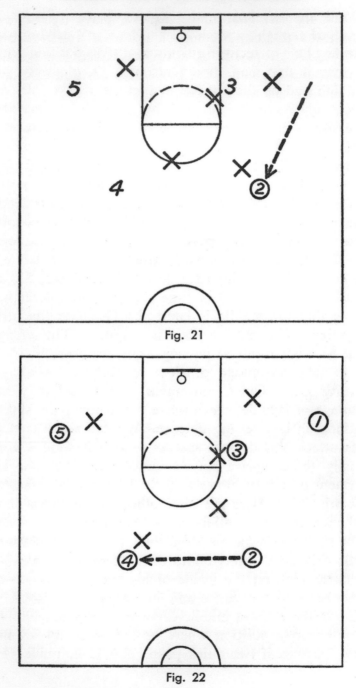

Fig. 21

Fig. 22

When the left guard receives, 4X plays tightly, overplaying the middle; 5X moves up to a quick recovery
position; 1X drops off to a two-pass recovery position;
3X maintains his same pass preventive position; 2X drops
back and toward the middle.

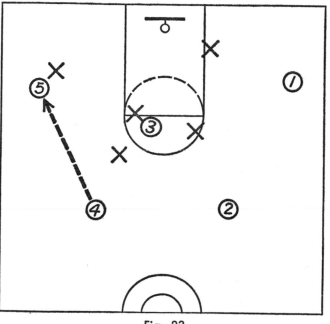

Fig. 23

The left forward has now received. Number 5X overplays the base line, 4X drops off to pinch the middle, 2X
drops off to a two-pass recovery position. Player 1X takes
the deep, weak side, and 3X takes his overplay position
on the post man. In giving these illustrations we have
not moved the post man around a great deal. Needless
to say, the offensive post man is not nailed to the floor.
So the defensive post man must be constantly shuffling
and moving to assume a stance that would prevent a pass
to the middle. There will be times when he would be in

great danger if a lob pass were thrown to his man breaking goalward. The best restriction on the lob pass to the post man is the deep sag man on the weak side—normally a defensive forward. When a lob pass is made he should yell "lob" and fade even more into the middle for (1) body checking action of the breaking post man, or (2) an interception of the pass.

The accordion action of sag, recover—moving in and moving out, onside and offside, by defensive men—requires a lot of *coordinated* and *cooperative* effort on the part of all five men. It requires constant verbal warnings of screens, lobs, cuts. It requires a team unity peculiar primarily to the sinking, switching, arm-waving, man-for-man defense.

There are two very difficult offensive maneuvers to defend against while using the sinking man-for-man. One of them is the set shot over a stationary screen. The other is the screen and roll.

Of course, the set shot over a screen can be prevented any time the defensive man is able to go over the top of the screen. If the screen is extremely tight and he feels the danger too great to go over the top, he may find his man stopping to shoot while he is momentarily blockaded by the screen man. To complicate matters further, his own teammate, defending the screen man, will sometimes get in his way. That is why this particular situation should be practiced as a break-down drill. It can be dealt with smoothly and efficiently if the players understand what they are dealing with and the method to be used.

In this situation, number 1 has passed to number 2, faked toward the middle, and stepped behind the stationary screen so tightly that the defensive man cannot get over the top. The result is a line up of four players, two offensive and two defensive. Some rule of thumb must be used

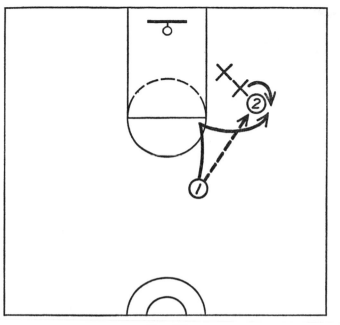

Fig. 24

to cover this play. Here is one such rule: THE NEAREST
DEFENSIVE MAN TO THE POTENTIAL SHOOTER MUST
CHARGE AROUND THE SCREEN ON THE BASE LINE SIDE.
He comes around on the base line side because that is the
most vulnerable position. If the lineup of players should
occur at the head of the circle and it is difficult to determine
which base line is nearest, the defensive man nearest the
ball simply comes around either side as shown in Figure 25.

If the ball handler drives toward the free throw line at
the moment his defensive man comes around, number 2's
defensive man, 2X, will take him, leaving 1X to cover
the potential roll-out man, number 2 (See Fig. 26).

This leaves 1X in what is apparently an indefensible
position. He is left trailing his man to the goal, and
vulnerable to a lob pass. He should crowd number 2 and
raise his arms high over his head and get his body between

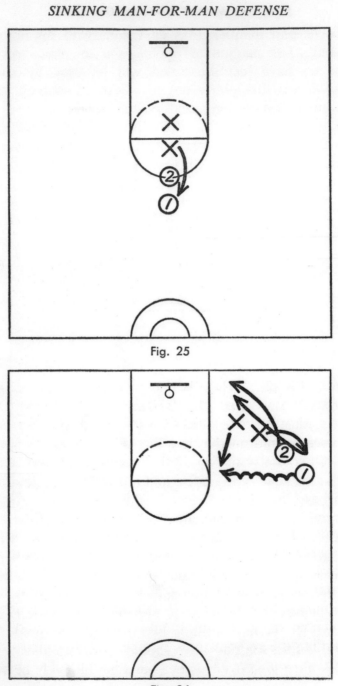

Fig. 25

Fig. 26

number 2 and number 1 as he breaks with his man for the goal. The method of playing the set shot over the screen we have just illustrated will be used by sliding teams—teams that *prefer* not to switch. Switching teams will want to handle the situation differently.

To use the switch, the defensive men will find themselves side by side at the crucial time of the shot over the screen.

Fig. 27

Player 2X would normally be waiting for the offensive man, number 1, to come around, at which time the switch will take place. In this case he must go around number 2 on the base line side—nearest number 1. Again, there is the danger that number 1 will drive opposite at that particular moment, leaving number 2X the defensive task of guarding the roll-out man, number 2. Of course, if he does drive, number 1X will pick him up. The biggest mistake most switching teams make in this situation is the failure of the deep switch man to come on around the stationary screen on the base line side.

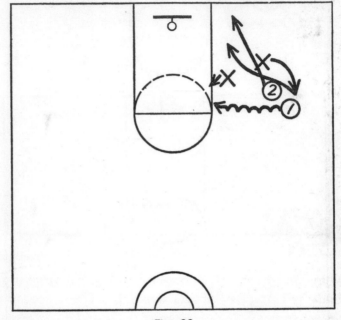

Fig. 28

The screen and roll presents a really challenging defensive play. If the defensive man could always get over the top of a screen, there would be no problem. However, we know there is no such thing as *always* in the game of basketball. We must prepare for every eventuality. In this case we will simply assume that X1 cannot get over the top of the screen set by O2.

This *forces* a switching situation. Player 2X must pick up O1, leaving X1 to play the difficult roll-out maneuver. To do this he will turn his back on the ball. He will raise his arms overhead, get as close to the roll-out man as

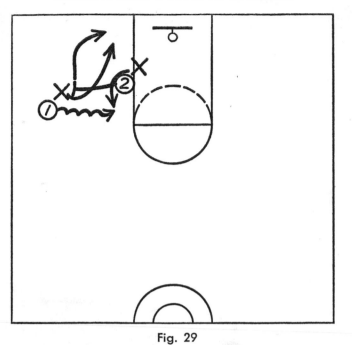

Fig. 29

possible, and break with him to the basket, making sure his body is between O2 and the ball. This appears to be an almost impossible defensive play to make. In actuality, it can be handled very nicely if the players are drilled and conditioned to respond.

If O1 should make his drive toward the base line, X1 can get over the top of the screen more easily if he has taken his normal base line overplay position. However, he could get screened in such a manner that he could not get over the top. In this case, the switch should become mandatory (See Fig. 30).

Here is the most important thing for defensive men to remember in playing the roll out. Raise both arms straight overhead and keep your body between your man and the ball to prevent the lob pass.

Fig. 30

To illustrate how the sinking, sagging man-for-man techniques we have discussed may be used, we will take a very popular offensive pattern and defend against it. The Drake Shuffle has become popular throughout the country. No doubt your team will be faced with the task of defending this continuity type offense several times during the course of a season. Here is the shuffle in its simplest form, showing continuity and the necessity for each man to know how to play each cut (See Fig. 31).

To play the first cut executed by number 3, 3X should go over the top of the screen set by number 5. He should not allow himself to be taken on the left side of number 5 as long as the ball is in the possession of number 2 or number 1. He should not get too far ahead of number 3 in playing 3's cut and he should not allow 3 to outrun him. He should keep his vision glued on number 3's

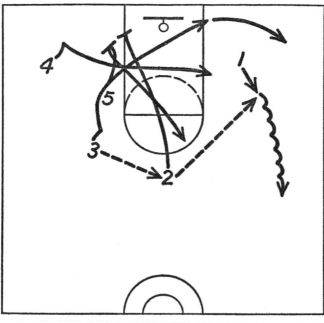

Fig. 31

chest, keep both arms up, and overplay his cut by half a man all the way to the goal (See Fig. 32).

You will understand that this makes a pass to number 3 at any time very hazardous. Number 3X is also close enough to body check in case 3 deviates from his normal route. The next cut is made in various ways by different teams using the shuffle. In this illustration we will show number 5 moving down the side of the key hole to set a screen on 4X, who should have assumed a deep sag position as soon as the ball was passed to number 1 (Fig. 33).

There is no need for 4X to attempt to fight over the top while playing number 4's cut. He knows number 4 wants to receive near the goal or in the pivot area. He must anticipate this move and be there waiting for number 4 to greet him on his arrival. If he should try to go over the top on this cut and the *pinch* is tight, he will get rubbed

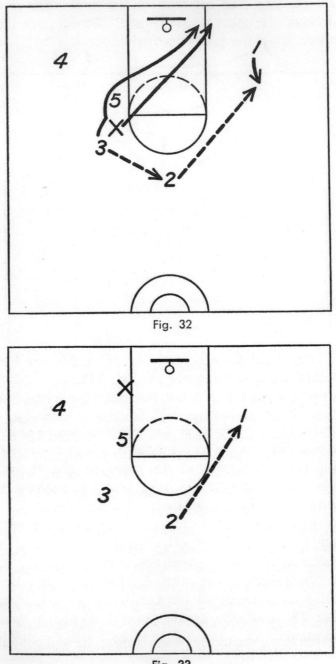

Fig. 32

Fig. 33

off and have to trail his man to the goal. The dangers
are obvious. He must be alert for a fake cut over the top
and break down the base line by number 4.

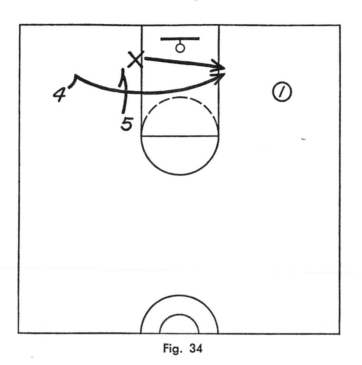

Fig. 34

Number 4 will try this if 4X overplays *too much*. The
defense of this cut is very simple if 4X is aware of this
possibility and doesn't turn his head to admire the ball
handling of number 1. He must keep his primary vision
focused on number 4 at all times (See Fig. 35).

The third cut is created by an interchange between
number 2 and number 5. Here is a situation that seems
to be defended best by switching, even though the ball is
not in the possession of 2 or 5. This area has become
congested as a result of the cuts executed by 3 and 4.
Number 2X is already standing where number 5 wants to
go and number 5X is already standing where 2 wents to go.
If the two defensive men simply exchange partners a

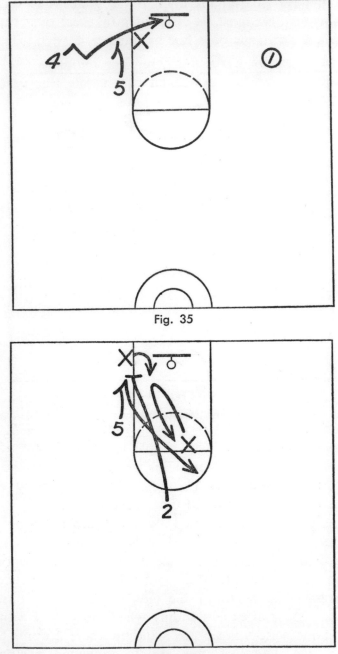

Fig. 35

Fig. 36

very difficult situation has been met simply and without complications (See Fig. 36).

Here is one offensive opportunity that makes switching hazardous on this particular play. The initial switch is not difficult and the defensive men can handle this variation if they are alerted to its possibilities.

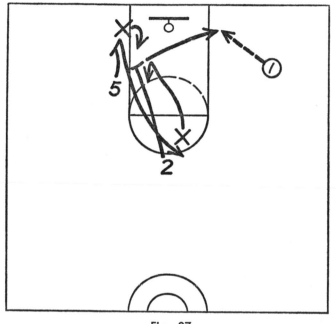

Fig. 37

The Drake Shuffle has many variations and options not shown here. These variations must be introduced to the defense and met by specific tactics. Drilling defensively against the shuffle makes use of all the principles of man-for-man play listed in Chapter 2. It illustrates how the middle can be jammed by sagging. To be successful, pressure must be put on the ball handler at each point. Good arm movement must be utilized to hamper passing. Rebound strength is good if the shot is taken at any one of the positions shown.

The greatest danger created by the use of sinking man-for-man tactics is human laziness. Sag men will be tempted to take advantage of the fact that their man does not have the ball and take a rest period.

Assuming that the team is sold on sinking man-for-man and well drilled on its principles, the number of shots attempted in the critical shooting area can be cut to a minimum.

PART III

Zone Defense

5

Standard Zone Defense

B EFORE ANY ZONE DEFENSE can be studied, we must understand that the word zone is not synonomous with immobility. In years past, zones defenses have amounted to little more than a cluster of men standing with arms outstretched. They had virtually no movement. They were not aggressive when guarding outside shooters. They waited for a shot to be taken so they could rebound and take off with the ball. Most zone defenses were employed so that defense would not be too strenuous. Teams that used this method wanted to save their energy for the fast break and offensive play.

The defense we will be describing (whether 1-3-1, 2-1-2, etc.) will be an aggressive, moving defense. It will not allow shots to be taken without restriction at any spot on the floor. It will be a moving cooperative effort. It will be a hard working defense with no regard for the conservation of energy.

Zone defense and man-to-man defense are much more closely related than most coaches or players realize. Guarding the man with the ball is precisely the same except that the guarding is a little tighter when the zone is used. Weak side defenders can afford to watch the ball more than the opponent, but they should know where all the offensive players are located. Without this knowledge they cannot anticipate offensive moves. Anticipation and quick movement are the keys to good zone defense.

Cutters should not be ignored just because the zone defense is being used. Playing the cutter well requires good anticipation and analysis of the play that is evolving. Generally, it is a good idea to play all cutters man-to-man until they reach the keyhole area and then return to normal position. Normal position will depend on where the ball is located.

When guarding the man with the ball the stance needs a slight adjustment. The feet should be wider and closer to the ball handler. Both arms should be windmilling for pass deflections rather than using the one-arm-up, one-arm-down stance of man-for-man play. The zone defender can afford to play tighter because if the man should drive past him, zone teammates are more alert to pick up his man. However, dribblers can hurt a zone defense. It is not good to allow dribblers to penetrate the zone. A defender guarding a man with the ball should make every effort to keep him from making progress goalward. Even so, the danger is not as great as it would be if the man-to-man were being used.

Fast-break teams try to break even faster when attacking a zone defense. Therefore, the defensive fast break is of the utmost importance if the zone defense is to be used successfully. If dribblers penerate the critical shooting area very often before the zone has an opportunity to *set up*, zone defense is worse than useless. The zone should be formed and set before a penetration is made. This gives each man an opportunity to analyze and anticipate the possible movements of the zone attack.

Some teams work assiduously on the rebound block-off position if they are using the man-to-man defense. Some of these same players will ignore the block off when they are zoning. The zone certainly enjoys a rebounding advantage, but the rebound block-off position should not be eliminated. If each offensive player will simply block out the nearest opponent, getting the rebound becomes a simple matter.

Any time the ball is passed to the pivot area or base line area near the basket, a zone defense must collapse to protect against this immediate threat. Therefore, it is well to remember when guarding passers, cutters, or dribblers, to anticipate passes to these areas. Do everything possible to keep the ball on the outside of the zone.

There are various rules of thumb used to determine when and where to use the zone defense. There are those teams who use it in the early season only. There are those who use it on the home floor only. It is our contention that such rules are designed with the assumption that good outside shooting will beat the zone. The type of zone defense we are advocating does not allow open outside shots. It is more positive to prepare a good, sound defense for use any time of the year on any floor. If it is to be weak in late season or inappropriate when playing away from home, then it is surely not reliable.

The 2-1-2 Zone

The 2-1-2 is one of the oldest zone defenses in basketball. Originally it was not very active and was designed primarily as a defense from which to fast-break. Various types of 1-3-1 offensive attacks have lessened its popularity in recent seasons. There is still an important place in basketball defense for the 2-1-2 zone.

The 2-1-2 is a good defense to use when an opponent has concentrated the major part of its offensive strength at one or both of the guard positions. The two front men of the zone can afford to pick the guards up tight and gamble somewhat, since the three deep men will be able to help them out in case of trouble. Of course, the 2-1-2 would work well against any offensive attack that is similar in nature. Any single post attack or overload box formation can be defended well by the 2-1-2. The 2-1-2 is certainly a fine concealment defense. That is, when a team is using a man-to-man and wishes to change to a zone, this defense can be used for several minutes before the offense realizes it is being zoned.

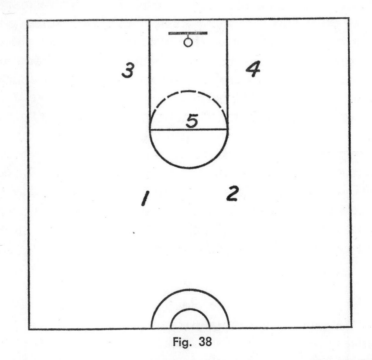

Fig. 38

This diagram shows the *initial* positions. Defenders 1 and 2 cue their positions off the key hole area. They do not want to become too widely separated. If they take positions on an imaginary line extended forward from each side of the key hole, they will have good communication with each other. Defenders 3 and 4 take the positions shown, but in the event the ball is in imminent danger of being passed to one side of the floor, the defender on that side moves out quickly in anticipation of the ball. They should line up fairly close to the 3-second area so that the zone will not be spread out for easy passes to the pivot. If offensive players line up behind them, they would back up half a step. When no offensive player is near the goal, they play as high as possible. The middle defender lines up on the free throw line. If it is necessary he will come even higher to overplay any offensive man in the pivot area. Any single offensive player in the pivot area should be defended by number 5, just as though he were using a man-for-man defense. The front two defenders should halt the progress of the ball down court—

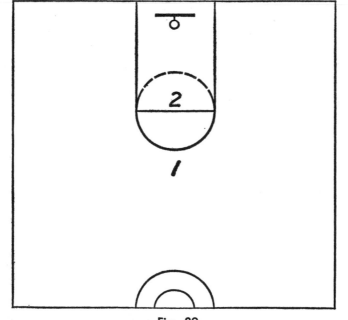

Fig. 39

the quicker, the better. To defend against the fast break, 1 and 2 may use a tandem position after racing back to the defensive end of the floor as soon as possible (Fig. 39).

If a real fast-break threat materializes, defender 1 stops the ball and defender 2 protects the goal. If no fast-break threat materializes, the tandem men will move out in the normal position as soon as numbers 3, 4 and 5 arrive.

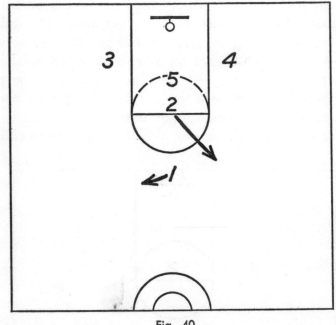

Fig. 40

Let's take a look at the 2-1-2 zone with the ball stationed at various positions in the front court. Movement of all five defenders begins as soon as the ball enters the front court (See Fig. 41).

The left guard brings the ball into the front court and immediately meets resistance from number 1. The other front defender fills in behind him to prevent a pass to the post area. The middle defender, number 5, moves in

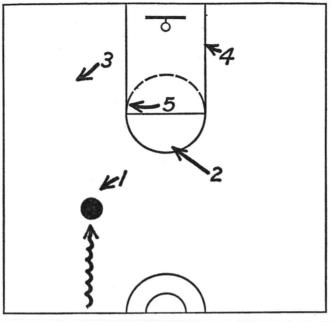

Fig. 41

to get in line with the ball and the goal. If an offensive man were in the middle he would play in front of this man. Number 3 moves outward to put pressure on any potential receivers in his side or corner area. Number 4 drifts goalward since the ball is two passes from his area.

If the ball is passed across the front court the action of numbers 1 and 2 will be just like that of the sinking man-for-man (See Fig. 42).

Number 2 comes out to meet the receiver and number 1 fills in behind him. Number 5 moves to get in line with the basket. Number 3 moves goalward and number 4 moves out to cover the passing threat to his area.

If the ball is passed to the side or corner covered by number 4, he covers the receiver. Number 4 overplays the baseline, as if he were playing man-for-man (Fig. 43).

Number 5 slides to a point about halfway between the

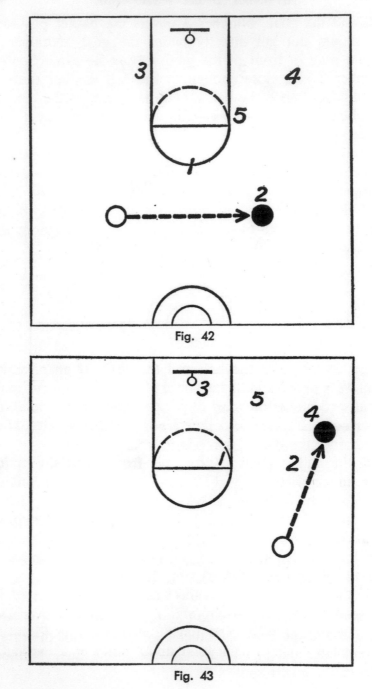

Fig. 42

Fig. 43

ball and the goal. Number 3 covers the basket position. He should not get directly under the goal. Number 3 should play in front of the goal so that he can rebound. Number 2 gets close enough to the ball handler that he could cover him if the ball should be passed to the corner. Number 1 fills toward the pivot area to help protect that vulnerable spot.

If the ball is passed to the corner, number 4 will release and cover that man while number 2 slides to fill the defensive position he vacates. If number 4 overplays the baseline vigorously, the ball will have to be floated to the corner, giving him plenty of time to get there before the receiver can become a scoring threat.

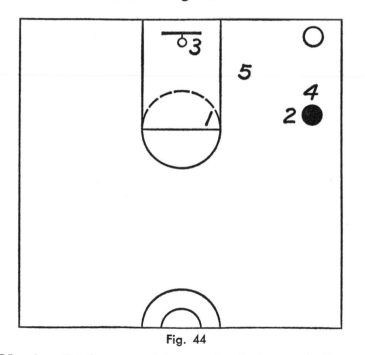

Fig. 44

Number 5 takes a position as the 2nd man in line with the ball and the goal. Number 1 gets outside of the three-second lane and just below the free throw line. Number 3 takes the goalie spot.

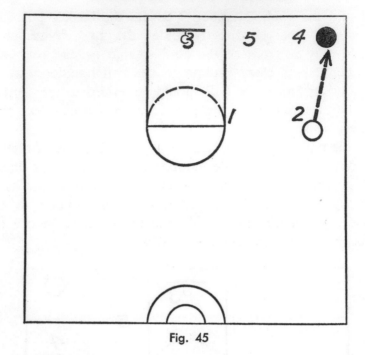

Fig. 45

At this point, the greatest danger is a pass to the key hole area. If an offensive man moves into the baseline pivot area, number 5 should step in front of him (Fig. 46).

If an offensive man moves into the key hole area on the side and there is no offensive man on the baseline, number 5 should not waste himself guarding the baseline. He should pinch outward two steps and, with the help from number 1, prevent the pass into the side post position (See Fig. 47).

With the ball at a position directly in front of the goal, number 1 and number 2 should pinch on the man with the ball and give him only poor passing lanes. The other men will keep their initial positions (See Fig. 48).

If the ball *should* be passed into the pivot area from a ball handler out front, he should get pressure from number 1, number 2, and number 5 (See Fig. 49).

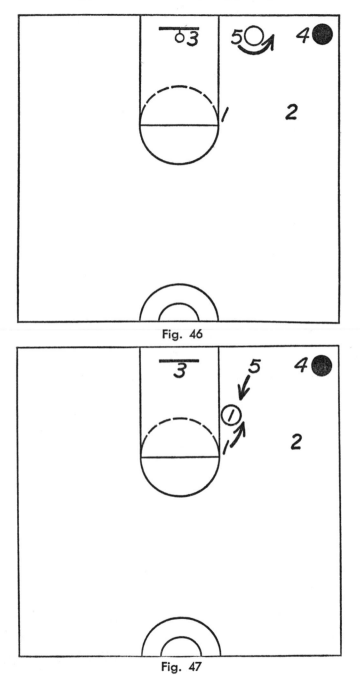

Fig. 46

Fig. 47

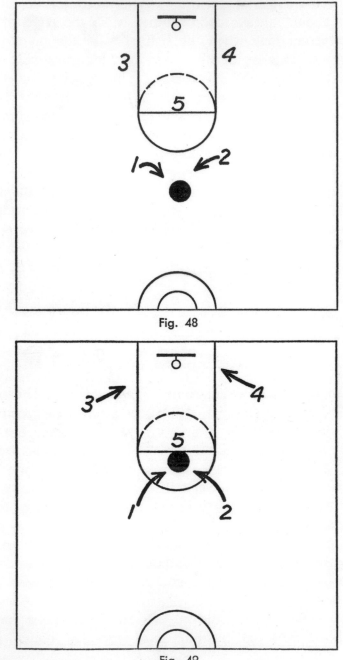

Fig. 48

Fig. 49

The main job is performed by the corner defenders. They should always drop off nearly to the edge of the three-second lane when the ball goes to the pivot from out front. This apparently leaves the wing spots wide open to receive from the pivot man. This is true, but those positions are not as dangerous as the pivot spot. There is also the threat of a pass to a baseline man from the middle if the wing defenders don't pinch toward the key hole and the goal. The best way to eliminate this threat is to keep the ball from going into the middle area.

The 2-1-2 slides shown to the right side of the floor would be made in just the same manner to the left side. Of course, the numbers and assignments would be reversed.

The 2-3 zone slides and principles are so much like those of the 2-1-2 that we will not show them. The only difference lies in the play of number 5 who has to go into the middle spot anyway if an offensive player is located there.

The 1-2-2 Zone

The 1-2-2 is an example of a point defense. That is, it would be most efficient against an offense that employs only one man in the offensive area in front of the free throw line. This does not mean it is impossible to use the 1-2-2 against a two-man offensive front.

The 1-2-2 appears weak in the middle. Actually, the only way the middle can be attacked successfully is for the pass to be made from a side position and the point man to react slowly. This defense offers great rebounding strength. A team with two big, strong rebounders may place them underneath the goal to insure the offense only one shot.

The point man should be fast and have quick hands. He should be a real hustling, hard working, "holler" guy.

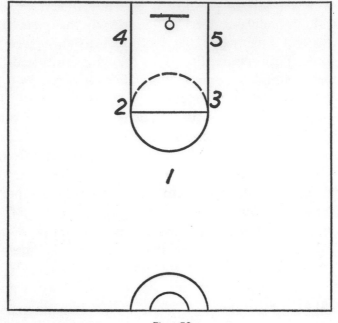

Fig. 50

Number 2 and number 3 should be quick with good arm movement. Numbers 4 and 5 need to be good, rugged rebounders. The 1-2-2 slides are relatively simple as long as the offense is a diamond formation or any other form of point offense. Here are the slides for the 1-2-2.

With the ball at point position, numbers 2 and 3 must be conscious of preventive passes into the post area (Fig. 51).

If a pass carries the ball to the right of the floor, number 3 moves out to cover the ball. The point man, number 1, drops toward the end of the free throw line on the side of the ball. Number 2 drops off toward the goal. Number 5 comes out so that he could cover the corner quickly if the ball were passed to that position. Number 4 comes across to the front of the goal (See Fig. 52).

When the ball goes to the corner, the ball handler is covered by number 5 (See Fig. 53).

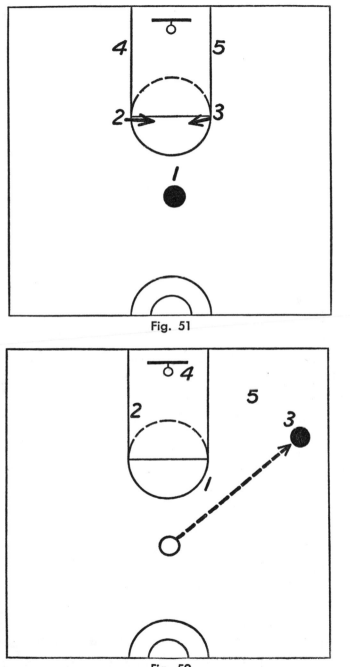

Fig. 51

Fig. 52

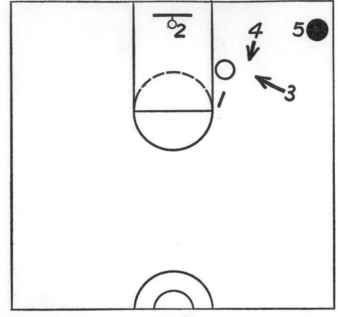

Fig. 53

The most vulnerable positions to defend are the positions on either side of number 1 when the 1-2-2 is in its initial set up. If two offensive players elect to pass the ball back and forth, they can harass number 1 greatly unless the 1-2-2 defends against this movement of the ball (Fig. 54).

As soon as the ball is passed to one of the ball handlers, the receiver should be covered by number 1 and a return pass overplayed. In this case, the left offensive guard receives. Number 1 covers and overplays a return pass. Number 3 moves up one step for a *threat* or possible interception if a lob pass is made to the offensive right guard. This rather forces the ball to go to the left side of the floor which resents no unusual movement for the 1-2-2 (Fig. 55).

If the ball moves to the offensive right guard, number 1 overplays and number 2 pulls out slightly for the interception or threat. Again the ball is forced to the right side of the floor and normal slides can be used (See Fig. 56).

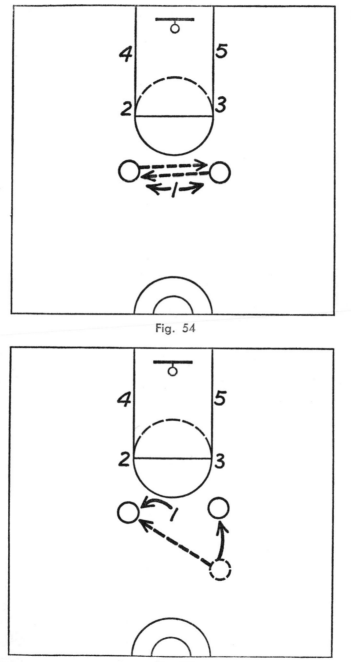

Fig. 54

Fig. 55

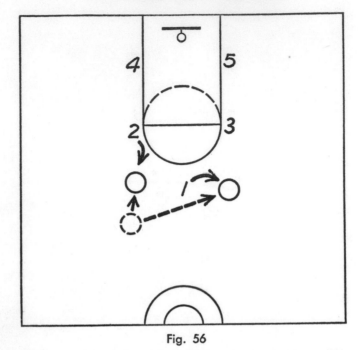

Fig. 56

Again, the slides have been shown with ball movement to the right side of the floor. These same slides would be used if the ball movement were to the left. The assignments would simply be reversed.

The 3-2 Zone Defense

The 3-2 zone defense is used primarily by offensive-minded teams. It seems contradictory to say, but the 3-2 is not really a defense but an offense. The fast-break team with two, big, rugged rebounders can employ a 3-2 zone as an offensive weapon. With two men under to get the rebounds and three men releasing, a fast-break offense can be generated very quickly (Fig. 57).

Against certain types of attacks, the 3-2 also poses a real problem. The three front men cooperate and move in such a manner that the offense is unable to determine whether the defense is a 3-2 or a 1-2-2. Obviously, the greatest

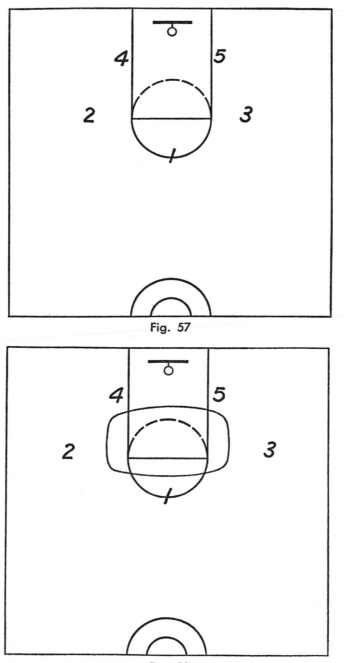

Fig. 57

Fig. 58

weakness lies in the middle area. If the middle man on the 3-2 can be a tall, fast man, the middle can be adequately covered (Fig. 58).

The two outside front men should be very fast and, needless to say, the two deep men should be big and strong, and excellent rebounders. Here are the slides for the 3-2.

Any time the ball goes to a side floor position, number 1 will protect the middle. He is the *primary* middle protector at all times. If the ball goes to the left side, number 2 covers the ball.

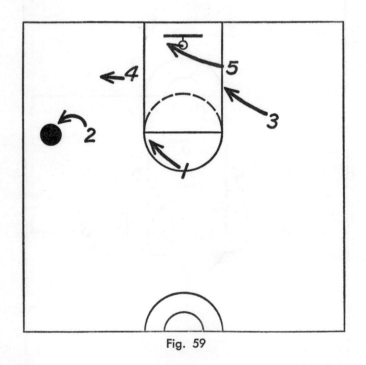

Fig. 59

Number 4 will have to cover the corner if the ball goes there so he is taking an advantageous position for moving to that spot. Number 3 will cover the goal if the ball goes to the corner so he is moving in that direction.

Number 2 should overplay the pass to the corner. The best rebounding occurs when number 4 and number 5 are under the goal. With the ball at a corner spot, only one of these big men are in position to rebound. However, if the ball does go to the corner (in this case), number 4 covers the ball.

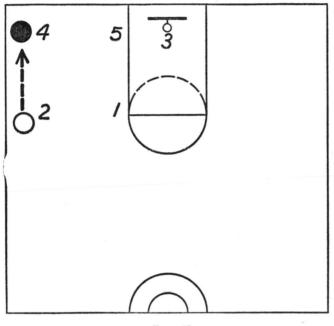

Fig. 60

Number 2 covers the outlet, number 1 protects the middle, number 5 is the second man in line with the goal, and number 3 is the goalie.

If the ball goes to the side post area, numbers 5, 1 and 2 pinch (See Fig. 61).

With the ball resting at a point position, the defense looks almost like a 1-2-2 defense. Number 1 makes every effort to prevent a pass from going into the middle (Fig. 62).

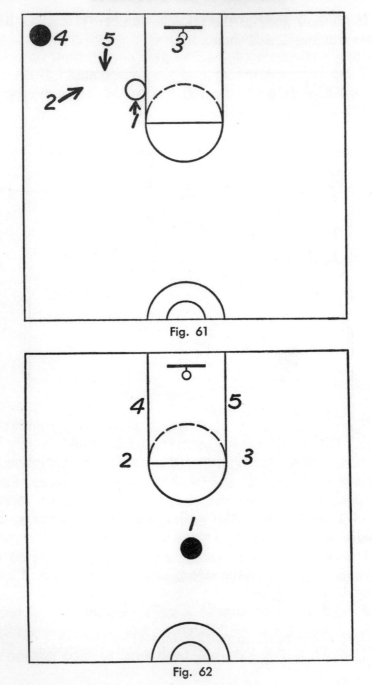

Fig. 61

Fig. 62

If the ball goes to the middle, number 1 receives help from number 2 and number 3.

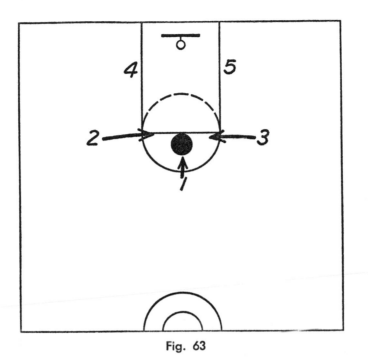

Fig. 63

The key to having a good 3-2 zone is the number 1 man. He should be big and fast. He should be big to prevent passes to the middle. Two good, rugged rebounders are necessary. If shots are taken from outside, there are generally only two men under, numbers 4 and 5. Number 1 should be excellent at diagnosing and analyzing offensive play.

The 3-2 slides to the other side of the floor would be the same with the assignments reversed.

The 1-3-1 Zone Defense

Here is the basic formation that gives the 1-3-1 defense its name. It is only a starting formation, because as soon as the offense crosses center line, the 1-3-1 will shift to meet it. This formation changes every time the ball moves even slightly. Three players are in line from side line to side line. Three are in line from center court to goal. The free throw line is used to key the lateral line on its position.

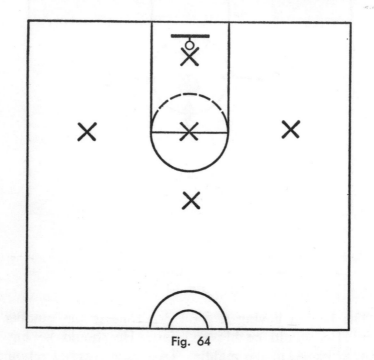

Fig. 64

There are five spots that each player must recognize and react to automatically. The first one is directly in front of the goal and may be anywhere from center line to free throw line. If the ball is in that area, the number 1 man takes the ball handler and the other players maintain basic positions, unless there is a receiver to overplay (Fig. 65).

Another spot that is defended by reflex action is the right wing position. The defensive wing player, number 3 on the right side, will overplay the pass to the corner. This half-step overplay also discourages a dribble by the ball

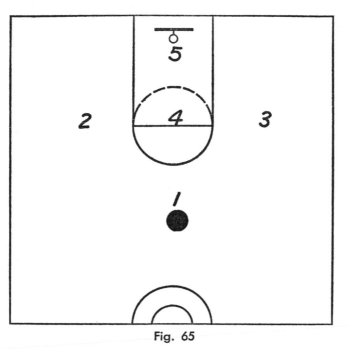

Fig. 65

handler. There are not three men in precise alignment with ball and goal. Number 4 is directly in line, but number 2 is in his secondary position and number 5 has started to "cheat" toward the corner in case the ball is passed there. Number 1 has floated to the free throw line to help clog the pivot area (See Fig. 66).

The right corner is defended by number 5. He has already "cheated" a little in that direction, but if the ball does get to the corner, he moves to guard that man strongly. Number 3 overplays a possible return pass to the wing, so that a high, long pass out to the front must be made. In that case, number 1 should be alert to intercept it. Number 4 has taken the second position, and number 2 has moved all the way in to a spot one yard in front of the goal. If the ball is passed to a corner, the offensive team should be stymied right there. It should never be allowed to get the ball out successfully.

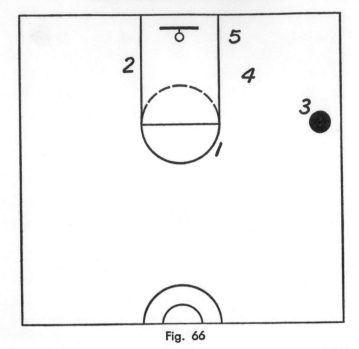

Fig. 66

The left wing defensive position is slightly different from the right wing, since number 4 plays the left corner. Too much burden is placed on number 5 if he has to play both corners. To alternate their assignments strengthens both positions, but it also causes each side of the floor to be played slightly differently. Number 2 overplays the ball handler; number 4 cheats one step toward the corner; number 1 has the free throw line; number 3 is moving toward the basket, and number 5 has moved one step toward the corner, since he will take the second spot if the ball does go to the corner (See Figs. 67, 68).

The left corner is also played differently from the right corner. Number 4 plays the ball handler; number 5 takes the second spot and number 3 has the goal. Number 2 overplays the pass out, and number 1 moves even closer to the middle. If a high long pass is made to get the ball

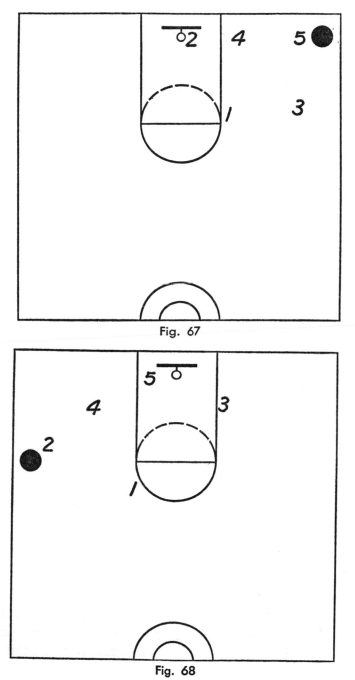

Fig. 67

Fig. 68

out of the corner, every one of the five defensive men moves
and moves fast enough to recover his original position.
Number 1 goes for the interception. The men know they
are going back to their original positions because they will
not allow the ball to be passed to the middle or back out
to a wing spot.

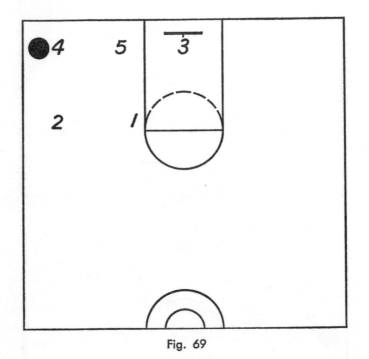

Fig. 69

There are two other positions that will have to be dealt
with. One is the middle or post area. The ball should not
be allowed to go there often. If it does, the middle man
will guard the ball handler strongly and every other defensive player will sag toward the middle and the goal at
the same time.

The point, or number 1 man, plays the ball any time
it is out front. If there are two players out there passing
the ball back and forth, the point man is put at a dis-

advantage. In that event, he will play only one of them while the offside wing man will come up as far as an imaginary line drawn across the floor from side line to side line and intersecting the head of the circle. The point man will play the man who is adjacent to the greatest accumulation of offensive strength. That is, he will play the man on the strongest side of the floor. The numbers 5 and 4 men will "flex" just a little, as shown in the diagram. These adjusted positions are held only as an initial position. As soon as the ball moves, regular or normal 1-3-1 positions will be taken. Wing men will never come higher or farther (See also Fig. 71) out than the dotted line.

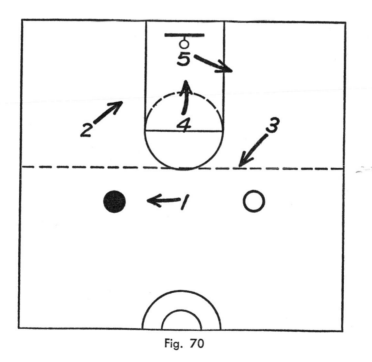

Fig. 70

1-3-1 Personnel Assignments.

The point, or number 1 player, should indeed be the team's number one defensive player. He should be fast,

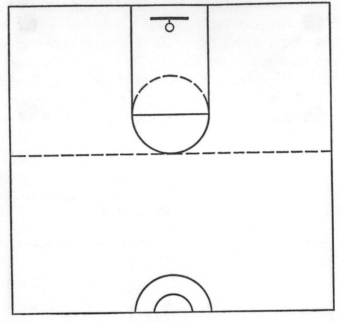

Fig. 71

intelligent, and a leader. He is a person who constantly harasses the opposition. Usually this man will be a guard. Number 1 has five basic positions to play. He should be drilled as an individual on these positions. The coach can put him at each spot and tell him the spot number. The coach can then stand at center court and call these numbers as signals. Here, illustrated, are the five primary spots. There will be other points for him to cover, but these five should be automatic for him. (The open circle is the ball and the dark circle is number 1.) The numbers are his signals (See Fig. 70).

The wing men, numbers 2 and 3, should be drilled together. They have an equal number of positions to play. Illustrated (Figures 73, 74) are the wing men, the primary positions for each spot and signals for each.

Note that on signals 1, 4, and 5, each man keeps his

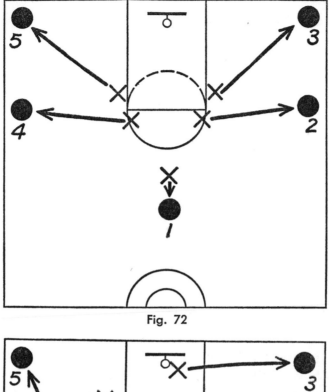

Fig. 72

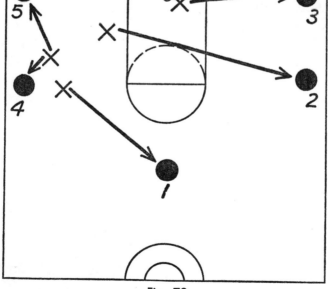

Fig. 73

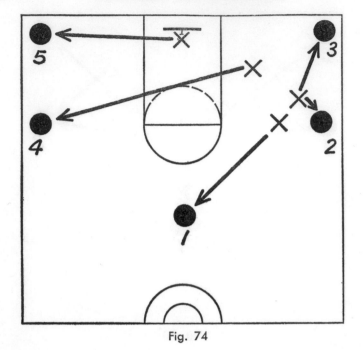

Fig. 74

normal wing spot. That is the biggest reason why your slowest men can be put at the wings. They are the easiest to play and require the least speed. If the team has a couple of boys who are otherwise pretty good basketball players but who lack speed for man-for-man defense, this zone might well be the defense for that team.

Player 4 should be the second best team defensive player, or first among the taller players. He has five positions to cover and he has a long way to travel in covering them. He must be fast, and he should be one of the taller players. Here are his spots and signals (See Fig. 75).

The goalie is usually your tallest player and the best rebounder. He is the second best big defensive player. The weakest guard and the weakest forward are usually put at the wings. The best tall man and the next best tall man are put at the middle and goalie positions. Your goalie

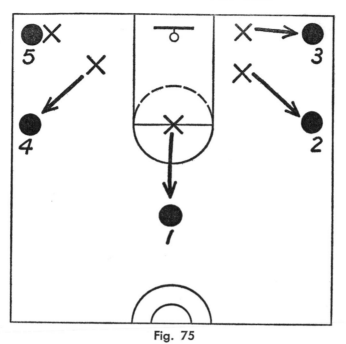

Fig. 75

should be in position to get the most rebounds. The wing men actually get more rebound opportunities than might be suspected of their second and third positions. The goalie need not be an exceptionally fast man. Here are his positions and signals. Players 4 and 5 might be drilled, on occasion, as a two-man drill (See Fig. 76).

After the players can cover these basic spots by reflex action, they need to work on the spots that could be termed *infrequent*. Defense for pivot play is infrequent because the ball should not be allowed to get in there very often. The spots on either side of number 1 are played only infrequently because most teams will run a one-man front offense against a one-man front defense. Even so, these spots must be faced on occasion. They need not present a great problem.

It is suggested that the coach *take* the ball to these spots

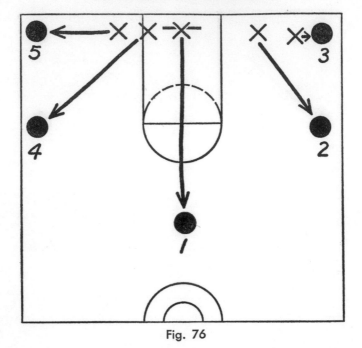

Fig. 76

and work all five men as a team. Each man will have to flex slightly out of the normal four or five spots he ordinarily has to play. He should consider it a gift when, in a game, a team takes the ball to one of his four or five regular spots. The number will vary according to position. Some players have an extra spot to play, as in the case of the middle man, number 4. It is suggested that you have a five-man drill of *regular* positions and a five-man drill on *infrequent* positions. They may be called Drills One and Two, or any other name (See Figs. 77, 78).

Teaching Hints

1. *It is better to teach one type of zone well than to attempt several in a haphazard manner.*
2. *Teach aggressive zone play. Give 'em nothing, anywhere, any time.*

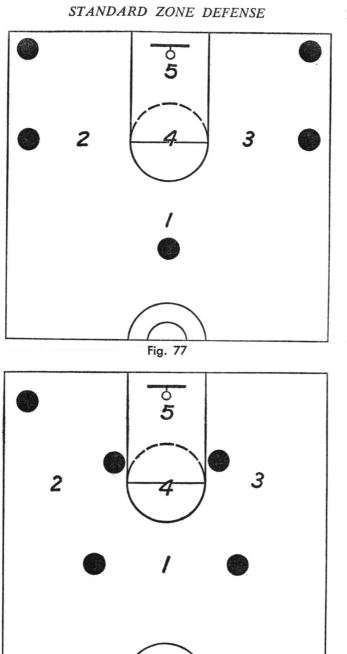

Fig. 77

Fig. 78

3. *Zone defense is not the defense for a lazy coach or team.*

4. *Stance is closer and feet are wider than in the man-for-man defense.*

5. *Overplay the passer and pass receiver. Don't allow them to move the ball freely.*

6. *Overplay the pivot. Do not allow the opposition to move the ball to that spot easily.*

7. *Don't congregate. Stay spread if there is no necessity of playing close to the man guarding the ball handler.*

8. *Never take a defensive position under or behind the goal. You are out of play.*

9. *Fast-break on defense. There is no excuse for any good defensive team giving its opposition a lay-up.*

10. *Do not give them the outside shot.*

11. *Be specific in teaching a zone defense. It's not* WHAT *formation you use but* HOW *you teach it.*

12. *Make personnel assignments according to position, size and abilities.*

6

The Matching Zone

THE MATCHING ZONE DEFENSE has evolved as one result
of the many offensive formations employed to attack zone
defenses. Obviously, it is futile to defend a 1-3-1 offensive
formation with a 2-1-2 defensive formation. For each zone
defense there is a counteroffensive formation to attack the
most vulnerable areas of the defense. Therefore the need
for a flexing zone defense that would "match up" a defensive player with each offensive player becomes apparent.
Assuming the offensive formation is more or less static,
the matching zone serves this purpose. If the offense has
little movement, the matching zone is at its strongest. Cutters moving through the defense and taking new positions
present the greatest threat to the matching zone.

This defense has one major ally—confusion. The offensive team whose zone attack is not versatile will become
confused and frustrated when the defensive formation
changes each time with the offensive formation change.
Confusion breeds lack of confidence. Lack of confidence
causes poor shooting, hesitancy, and poor ball handling.

The initial setup for the matching zone may be any formation you desire. Possibly the best formation to use on the first defensive play is one corresponding to what you expect from the offense. In other words, if they use a single post, traditional 2-1-2 formation, you may set up initially in a 2-1-2 defensive formation. If they use a 1-3-1 tandem offensive system, you may set up in a 1-3-1.

Let's assume you elect to start in a 1-3-1.

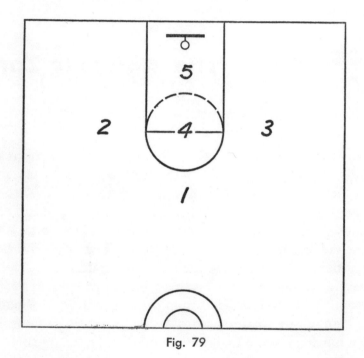

Fig. 79

The offense also uses a 1-3-1 formation (See Fig. 80).

As long as both offense and defense take this shape, man-to-man principles can be used more than zone. A real stand-off will result unless the offense sends cutters through or assumes another formation. If the offense elects to go into a 1-2-2 attack in order to concentrate strength around the number 5 man, little adjustment is required for your matching zone to fit the shape of the offense (Fig. 81).

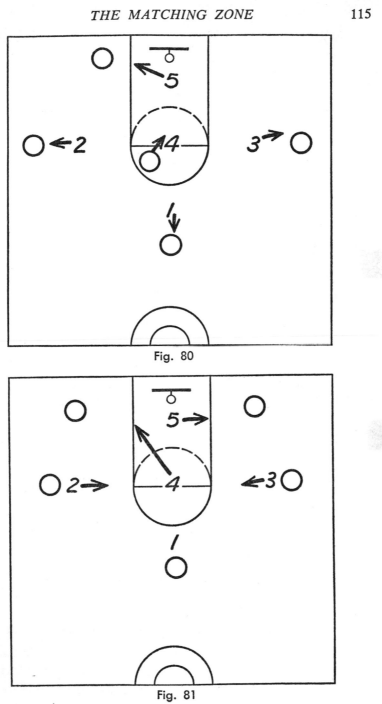

Fig. 80

Fig. 81

These movements are all common sense and natural. If number 4 leaves the middle area, numbers 2 and 3 are going to pinch inward. Number 4 should always drop diagonally to his right and goalward each time the offensive pivot area is not occupied. This will be number 5's cue to move to his left and take a position at the edge of the three-second lane. This flexing should not require a verbal signal from the coach or any of the players. It begins with number 4's adjustment when he finds no offensive threat in the pivot area. He may call "flex" or "adjust," but all five men should be drilled to such an extent they react automatically to various offensive formations.

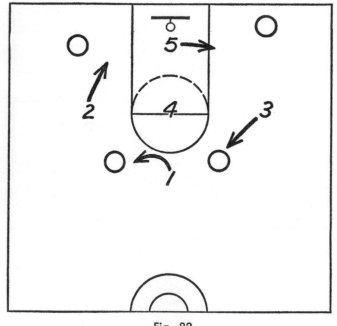

Fig. 82

If the offense elects to attack the 1-3-1 with a 2-1-2 formation, number 3 becomes the man to initiate the adjustment. Number 3 will move out and toward the head of the circle two full steps, number 1 will concentrate his attention on the offensive man to his right; number 2 will drop off two steps toward the goal and the three-second lane; number 5 will take his normal adjustment position, and number 4 will stay in the middle as long as an offensive man is in that spot. You will see that 1, 2, 5, and 3 have all simply moved two steps in a clockwise manner. This adjustment should always be initiated by number 3. His cue to make this adjustment is given by the offense. They give him his signal by concentrating two offensive players on number 1.

The *slides* should always be consistent. If you elect the initial position of a 2-1-2 zone, 2-1-2 slides should be used. If you elect the initial position of a 1-3-1 zone, 1-3-1 slides should be used. Assuming that we are using 1-3-1 slides and the initial position of the 1-3-1, let's see what movement our defense would take if the offense uses an overload formation.

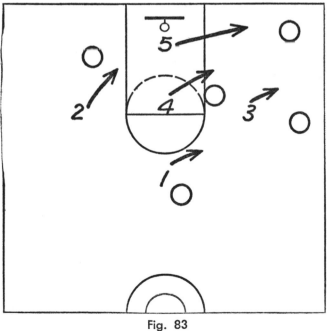

Fig. 83

It is number 5's normal duty to cover the corner to his left. Number 4's normal position any time the ball moves to the right side of the floor is half-way between the goal and the ball. Number 3 always protects the point, and number 2 starts toward the goal any time the ball starts toward the other side of the floor. If the offensive overload should move to the left side of the floor, normal 1-3-1 movement would be brought into play.

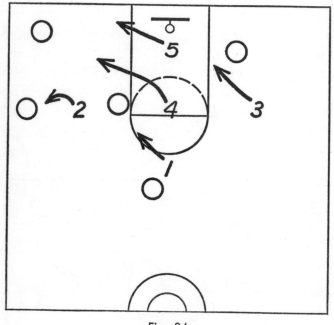

Fig. 84

Number 4 covers the corner normally so that when the ball goes to the corner, he would take that spot. The only teaching point you need to remember covers the situation with the ball at the left wing or left corner. With the ball at the left wing, numbers 4 and 1 pinch the offensive post man (See Fig. 85).

With the ball in the corner, number 5 and 1 pinch the post man (See Fig. 86).

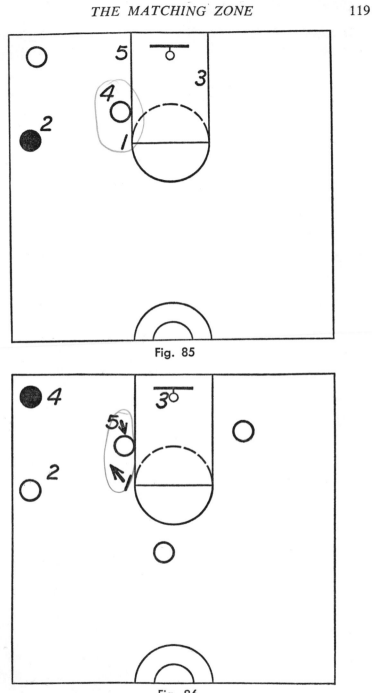

Fig. 85

Fig. 86

If you will take a close look at the 1-3-1 slides shown in the preceding chapter, you will see that we have deviated only minutely from normal movement to cover a multitude of offensive formations. If these offensive formations change shape rapidly however, and if there are continuous offensive cutters moving through the defense, the matching zone principles shown here are seriously threatened.

Teaching Hints

1. *Teach explicitly the formation and slides of one particular zone defense.*
2. *Learn the adjustments necessary for one particular offensive formation.*
3. *Teach the other adjustments necessary very slowly and very specifically—day-by-day—week-by-week.*
4. *Be sure the adjustment cues are understood.*
5. *Spend most of your time adjusting to the formation that presents the greatest threat to your matching zone.*
6. *Be sure the confusion is reserved for your opponent.*
7. *No defense can be executed well unless it takes shape before the offensive arrives.*
8. *No defense is of any value without dedicated, arm-waving, hard-working, cooperative, defensive-minded athletes.*

7

Pressure Zone Defense

A NUMBER of good zone pressure defenses are currently being used. Zone pressure has become more popular than man-for-man pressure in recent years. Of all pressing defenses we have personally observed during the past two seasons of play, man-for-man was used only twice. There are a number of sound reasons for this swing to zone pressure.

Nearly every basketball team has one good ball handler and dribbler. The one-on-one created by man-for-man pressing tactics offers the offensive player an advantage. He knows what he wants to do with the ball. If his teammates clear out and give him plenty of operating room, he can whip a very good defensive man.

Zone pressing tactics create better fast-break opportunities after ball possession has been gained. There are two, three, and often four men in position to break quickly and gain the jump on the team being pressed.

Zone pressure gives the team with one or two big, slow men an opportunity to be of value to the press. They will become rebounders and goalies. Man-for-man pressing tactics could not include such men because of the necessity for speed.

Zone pressure gives individual team members an opportunity to specialize. Defensive players develop special talents for different phases of the game, just as offensive players become more adept at certain skills. For instance, one boy will be the best at double teaming. Another will develop into the best ball hawk or interceptor. Another will become a specialist in diagnosing offensive play. If zone pressing tactics are used, each of these men will have an opportunity to exploit their special talents to the fullest advantage. Five small, fast men are not necessary to perform the zone press as is often true with the man-for-man press.

More organization is required of the zone press. Coaches have begun to use more offensive organization and they are eager to use their organizational ability on defense. Teams have developed special trademarks of defense, using various types of zone presses.

The history of sports is full of upsets. Upsets are created by unusual effort and a willingness to work *together*. This type of unity is epitomized by zone pressure defense. . . . Think of the greatest upsets you have witnessed and many of them were victories gained by the surprise of having to face a press. We have won two games in recent years after trailing by more than five points with two minutes to play. In each case the press won for us.

The press is a positive approach. If your team is definitely outclassed, it is your responsibility as the coach to *do something*. Obviously, you cannot go into the game and participate. One *thing* you *can* do is press. This is an example of doing something. A coach should never sit quietly and assume that he is outmanned and that defeat is sure when the opponent has stronger players. This same coach will surely lose games when he actually has stronger personnel. Therefore, pressing is positive. It is unifying. The players are enthusiastic about pressing. They feel in this way they can do something to offset the unequal balance of power. They feel they have a chance using these aggressive tactics to redeem an apparently lost game. They will have a good feeling even in defeat if they have given their all.

When should the press be used? Should we press only when we are behind? Should we press only when we are outmanned? It seems pretty apparent that there is no rule that can be used as the total answer. Here are some situations where the press might be utilized.

The press may work as a worthwhile surprise element early in the game. A quick press at the opening whistle for a few minutes might swing a lost cause to a victory. It might cause a superior opponent to *tighten* up and to begin making errors that continue even after you remove the press. This is especially true when defending the mechanical team that uses set plays.

The press is often effective when used during the last two minutes of the first half whether your team is ahead or behind in the score. In view of the fact that your team will be headed for the dressing room and a rest very shortly, they can put every ounce of energy into a fanatical defensive effort. So—the press is effective as a surprise tactic at the beginning or at the end of any period of play—for a short interval.

The most obvious time to press is late in the game when the opposition is ahead. I cannot think of a time when it is appropriate to play out a losing game until the final buzzer without attempting pressing tactics. This is a time for a team to pull together in a combined effort for the type of victory that breeds champions. A champion must be able to win (1) on the road, (2) with substitutes in the lineup, and, (3) when behind. Some teams are strictly front runners. That is, they play well as long as the score is in their favor, but when the score swings in favor of the opposition, they fall apart.

How long can the press be used? The answer to this will depend on the physical condition and ability of the team. Some teams are in such poor condition, they should never attempt to press. Other teams that achieve a high degree of stamina and physical condition should use the press in virtually every game for a goodly part of the game. Of course, an effective press for two or three minutes is much more valuable than a dogged half-effective press for twenty minutes. The press has been used successfully by some teams for the length of the entire game. It is doubtful whether a continuously winning ball club will ever need the press for more than a half.

In general, we might say it is time to begin thinking of the press *any time* your team falls behind by as much as 15 points.

Another general rule of thumb would be to employ the press any time your team is behind by as much as 10 points with 8 minutes to play. A sound rule is difficult to define. So many factors will determine the use of the press that use of a rule could become a negative factor.

Every effort should be made to make the press a surprise. The press may be put on by prearranged cues defined before the team takes the floor. It may be put on by prearranged signals from the bench. It may be put on by prearranged signals from the floor captain. It is imperative that all five men know precisely when and how they are to press. If one man fails to get the signal, the entire team effort will be lost.

Other than surprise, one of the best weapons the pressing team has at its disposal is the nervous system of the human body. This nervous system controls the skeletal framework, the muscular system, the circulatory system, the respiratory system—all of the physiological functions of the human being. Glands give off secretions that radically affect finely-drawn, delicately-balanced skills. The pressing team should make every effort to capitalize on this factor. They should yell, scream, fake, harass, talk, worry, annoy, and bully the opposition into such a state of frustration that they will be willing to give up the ball just so the turmoil will be ended.

Condition is a big factor in determining the success of a press. Pressing condition cannot be achieved by playing half-court basketball. It cannot be achieved by practicing the press once a week. Vigorous, strenuous, pressing drills should be used every day. One high school coach told me that his team uses the football field to practice the full court press. Of course, this work is done during the early fall when the weather is still mild. Bar bell training using the overload principle and track training using the over-distance technique were successful methods. Needless to say, this coach's team achieved the maximum physical stamina.

We will offer one type of zone press. The principles and system may well be utilized by any particular alignment of men you choose. The press explained and illustrated here will be the full and half court 1-2-2 zone press.

Let's take a look at the total floor space and get general perspective first.

There are certain areas more valuable for use by the pressing team than others. The side line and the corners provide the zone press with excellent double teaming opportunities. We have already shown these areas in the chapter dealing with man-for-man pressing tactics. One other factor enters into utilization of floor space when using the zone press: positioning of the referees. On every floor and in every league in the country, two officials are used. One leads the way down the right side line, turns the corner, and covers the area on the base line immediately under the goal. The other official is known as the trailer. He comes down the left side of the floor and, operating near the corner at center court, covering the area of play out front.

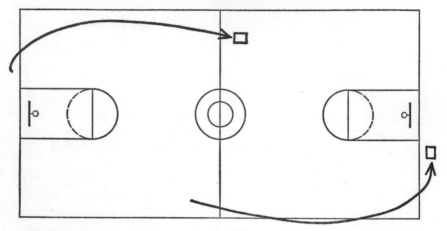

Fig. 87

This leaves a large portion of the front court area that neither official can cover fully. We are not advocating anything that is unsportsmanlike or anything that is unfair. However, if you had your choice of creating an aggressive double team situation right under the nose of either official or in the checkered area, illustrated in the diagram, which would you choose? Officials have an unwritten code they follow in calling fouls. They call only what they actually see. If an official is standing on top of a double team play, he can see more than if he is standing across the floor—a distance of 25 or 50 feet.

Let us say then that we are striving to gain a double team situation on the right side of the floor, preferably at or near the mid-court line.

To double team at the mid-court line takes advantage of the natural hesitancy many offensive players have when they reach that area.

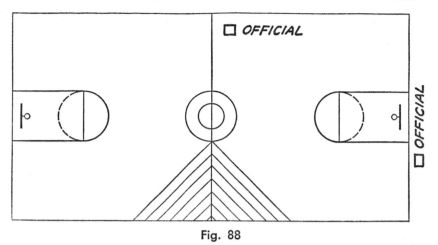

Fig. 88

We are not going to strive for a jump ball situation. We will be happy to tie the ball up, but we would much prefer to make a pass *interception*. To do this, we must first halt the progress of the ball, gain a vigorous, aggressive double team situation, and have a fast interceptor in position to *anticipate* the pass of the man being double teamed.

Our initial setup looks more like a 1-2-1-1 rather than a 1-2-2.

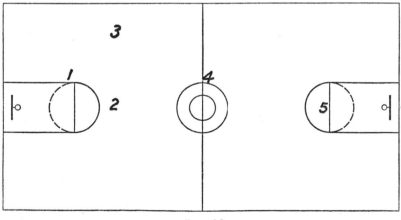

Fig. 89

Number 1 should be the fastest man on the squad. Size would also help since he will be involved in double teaming. He is the defensive *chaser* at all times. Number 2 is called the *double teamer*. He will be involved with number 1 in most of the double team situations. He needs to be fairly quick with good defensive arm movement. Number 3 is the *interceptor*. He plays in the most advantageous positions after a double team has been established. He should be a daring, aggressive individual who is keen on play analysis. Number 4 will eventually become a *corner man*. On this full-court initial setup, his job is to intercept long passes only. If the ball has progressed down-floor, number 4 will retreat into the right side of the key in order to cover the right corner area.

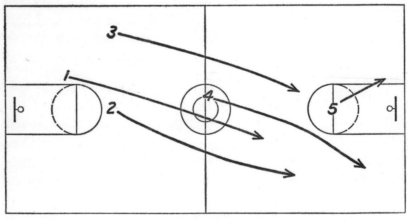

Fig. 90

Number 5 is the *goalie*. He sets up in front of the basket on the initial setup. He shouldn't get so close to the goal that he is wasted. He flexes backward to cover the left corner if the offense successfully gets the ball into the front court area. He will cover the left side of the goal and the left corner, according to the movement of the ball.

The zone press starts before the offense throws the ball

inbounds. Number 1 guides the ball into the right side of the floor if at all possible. Number 2 and 3 will help him somewhat with this objective by overplaying and *showing* the ball handler a receiver inbounds on the right side.

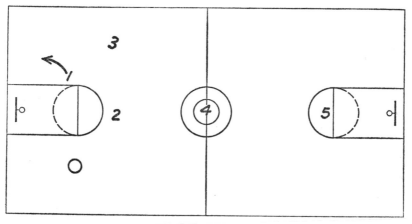

Fig. 91

If the ball is passed into the right side, the first objective has been reached and the 1-2-2 zone press can swing into action. Number 2 must cut off the attempted drive of the inbounds receiver. He should guide the dribbler toward the right side line and halt his progress as soon as possible. It would be ideal if this progress were halted near the midcourt line. While number 2 is stopping the dribbler, number 1 is in pursuit (See Fig. 92).

During number 1's chase, he wants to close the gap toward the middle of the floor so that the dribbler cannot escape in that direction from number 2. Number 3 observes the chasing and double teaming action very closely. He tries to determine who the ball handler will select as his receiver. When he has reached this decision, he tries to station himself in such a manner that he can intercept the pass. While establishing his position from which to intercept, number 3 should use fakes with the body, hands, and

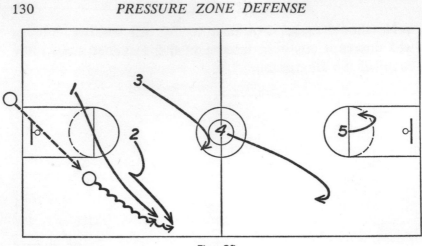

Fig. 92

arms. If he feels sure he knows where the pass is going, he should watch that receiver with split vision rather than letting the ball handler know he is aware of the receiver's position. Number 4 starts his movement toward a corner position, but halts when he is not quite halfway there. He will turn around and close the receiving area down the side line to his left with use of head fakes and body movement.

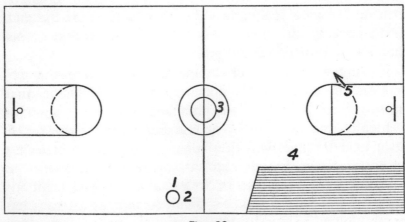

Fig. 93

He should make it obvious to the ball handler that he will intercept anything thrown in the darkened area indicated in the diagram.

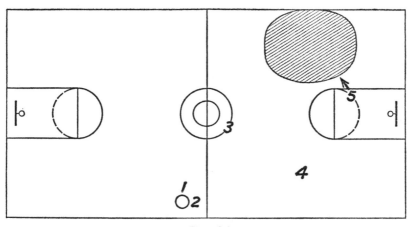

Fig. 94

It appears that number 5, our goalie, is doing a good deal of gambling. Actually, he should watch the goal with his primary vision and the darkened area with his peripheral vision. He should not leave his deep position until he is sure the double team situation has been achieved. He should not leave his deep position if there is an offensive man on the base line or in the corner covered by number 4. He should not leave his free throw line position unless the pass is thrown high and slow.

If number 5 or number 4 moves for the long pass interception, the goal will be immediately covered by the one not involved (See Fig. 95).

Ideally, the interception would be made by number 3 at or near the middle of the floor. He should be breaking as he intercepts and a quick fast break initiated with the cooperation of numbers 1 or 2. Because of player positioning on the floor it would be difficult to achieve a three-lane break. Number 4 will fill the right lane as fast, and,

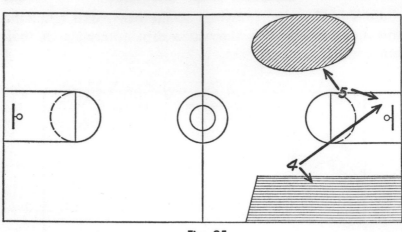

Fig. 95

as soon as he is sure number 3 has the ball. He will get there in time occasionally. Number 2 or number 1, whichever is not involved in the break, will move in as a trailer. Number 5 is a safety man in case the ball is intercepted or lost. His job is to protect the goal if such an event occurs. If the fast break two-on-one or three-on-one is not achieved and the pressing team moves into its regular offense, number 5 will move on down court.

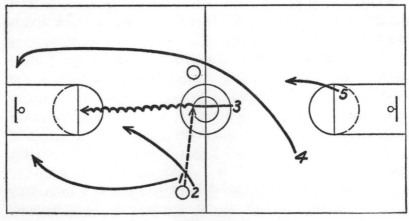

Fig. 96

Let's look at the press on a half-court basis assuming the offensive team has been successful in moving the ball into their front-court area.

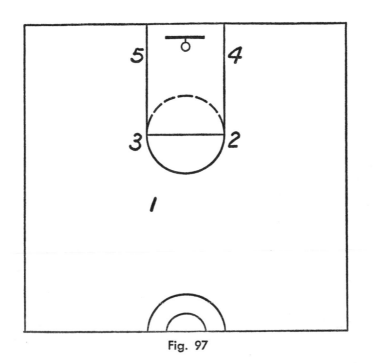

Fig. 97

Our defense now takes on more of the appearance of a 1-2-2. Notice that number 1 overplays to his right to guide the ball into the right side of the floor. We are still looking for a double team between number 1 and number 2 near mid court. Number 3 is still the interceptor. Number 4 will cover passes down the right side of the floor. Number 5 moves up when the double team is achieved to make passes into the middle area very dangerous. Number 3 covers the rest of the floor looking for interception (Fig. 98).

If number 4 and number 5 are fairly tall and keep their arms up, passes behind them to the base line area become very difficult. Too, we are assuming that since the ball

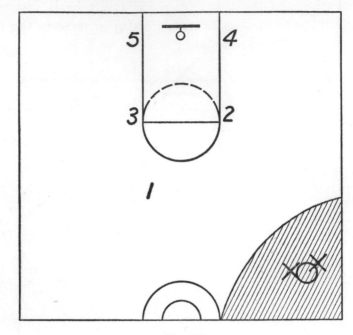

Fig. 98

handler is double teamed, a pass to that area must be high and slow, giving numbers 4 and 5 time to retreat quickly to either side of the goal (See Fig. 99).

If the double team is not achieved in this ideal situation, two policies may be pursued. (1) You may elect to play a normally aggressive 1-2-2 zone defense until the ball goes back to the good double team area when the press will be initiated again. (2) You may continue the 1-2-2 zone press all over the half floor with assignments reversed if the ball goes into the left side or left corner (See Fig. 100).

Let's assume you elect to stay with pressing tactics all the time. If the ball goes into the right corner, number 2 follows it in and looks for the double team with number 4. Number 3 watches the middle area; number 1 watches all of the release area, and number 5 protects the goal (Fig. 101).

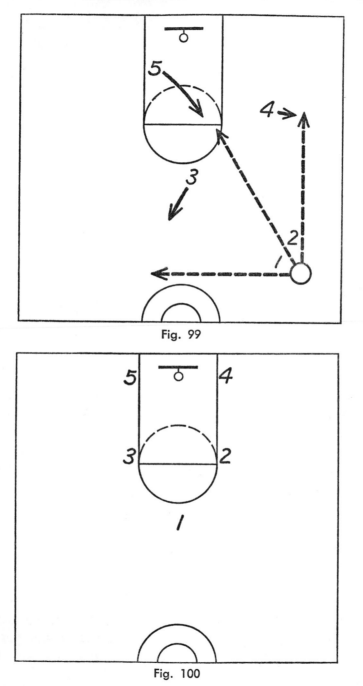

Fig. 99

Fig. 100

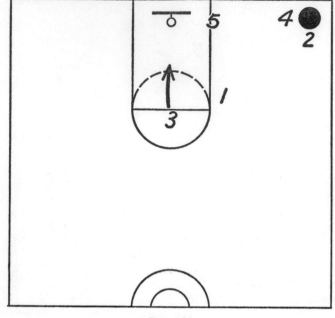

Fig. 101

If the ball should go into the left side, number 3 and number 1 become double teams, number 2 the interceptor, number 4 and number 5 swap assignments (See Fig. 102).

Fig. 103 is the left corner position. Number 3 chases the ball to the corner; number 1 covers the release out area, number 4 takes the goal, and number 2 covers the middle.

It is imperative that the chaser keep the ball on the right side of the floor the greatest percentage of the time. Once the double team has been achieved, the three remaining men *must* react quickly and efficiently to their tasks.

Teaching Hints

1. *Be sure each man has a precise knowledge of what is expected of him as an individual and as a member of the team.*

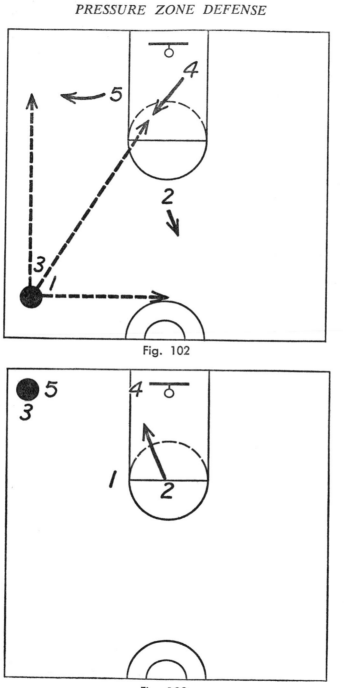

Fig. 102

Fig. 103

2. *Give each man a name such as interceptor, goalie, etc.*

3. *Practice double teaming each day as a break-down drill.*

4. *Don't allow indiscriminate fouling in practice sessions. Indiscriminate fouling will become your speciality.*

5. *Use the score board and clock when you practice the team press.*

6. *Develop rivalry and aggressiveness between teams when you practice.*

7. *Work on the press every day during early season practice. It will help develop good physical condition.*

8. *Don't always use the press simply as a last resort. It can be vital for use as a demoralizer of set-play opponents.*

Part IV

The Defensive Revolution

8

Combination Defenses

THERE IS A GROWING TREND toward stunting defense. A combination of zone and man-for-man tactics is one of the oldest types of stunting methods. The major objective is to confuse the offensive team and force them into a game they do not desire to play. "Make them play your game" is one of the oldest truisms. If an offense is allowed to run its plays or patterns just as they have practiced them, they are surely going to win. They should always be pushed out of their practices routines as much as possible.

Combination defenses are especially valuable in forcing pattern teams into another game. The new routes may be very good and very dangerous to the defense. Even so, the offense will rarely perform well running new routes or using adjustments necessitated during the course of a game. They will rarely perform well using moves or position play that has not been practiced. The combination defense must admit that there is an offensive answer. The percentages should be figured closely. Will this team that is stronger than mine whip us more easily running its favorite routes, or with forced routes created by an unusual defense? The answer is obvious. Here is another example of the time a coach can do *something*. It might well be dangerous. It is possible there are better things he can do. Still, he is doing something. He is not sitting back assuming that the stronger team always wins. Combination defenses are not reserved for the time when the opponent is stronger. You might use it when you are actually the strongest.

The Triangle and Two.

We will call this first type of combination defense the triangle and two. The triangle is created by the zone play of the three deep or base line men.

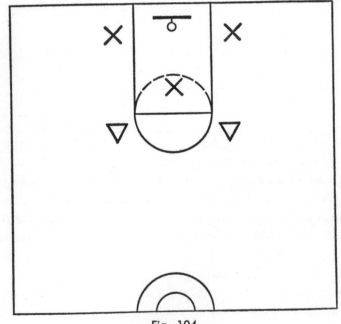

Fig. 104

The two front men will play their opponents all over the half-court using man-for-man techniques (See Fig. 105).

The *triangle and two* is more effective when the offense has not recognized the defense. Of course, they will recog-

Fig. 105

nize it sooner or later but the later—the better. You can help conceal what you are doing by having the front two men press as soon as the ball crosses center line. The back three men should stand near the offensive men nearest their positions so that they think they are also being played man-for-man. Once the ball has penetrated the front court area, the three deep men drop off to their zone spots while the other men continue playing man-for-man (Fig. 106).

The three deep men are left to cover the entire base line and middle area. Of course, the other two men will congest those areas since their men may be moving in and out. The greatest danger to the triangle and two is the use of clear outs by the offense.

Let's assume the offense either does not recognize the defense or does not know how to attack it. The three deep

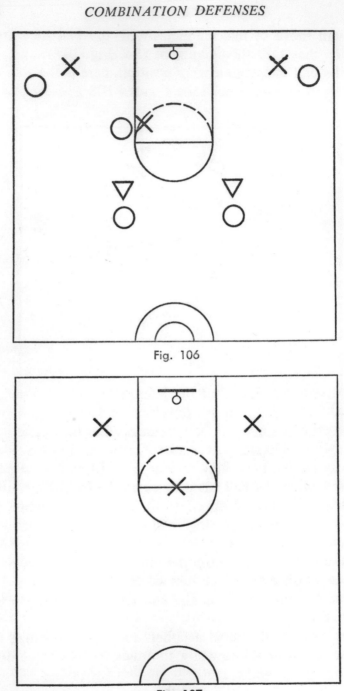

Fig. 106

Fig. 107

men will move in this manner. With the ball at a front position they take this alignment (See Fig. 107).

If the ball moves to a wing position, here is the way the three deep men operate. (See Figures 108 and 109).

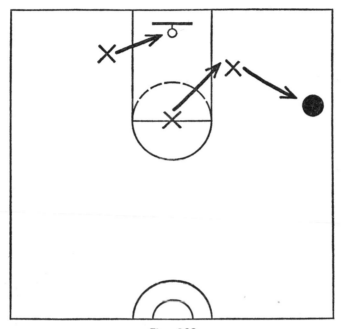

Fig. 108

The zone men cover these positions if the ball goes to a corner (See Figs. 110, 111).

The two men operating on man-for-man principles must go with their men. They should use sagging tactics whenever possible. The sag man should move out and pick up his man tightly as soon as he receives.

Ideal physical talent for this defense would be three tall, strong, zone men and two very fast front men. The defense can be used as an opener and then changed as soon as the offense recognizes it. If you move the front men to certain positions on the floor, you will see that the offense can cre-

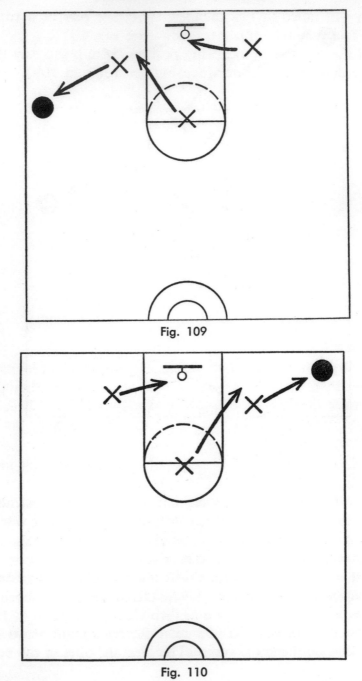

Fig. 109

Fig. 110

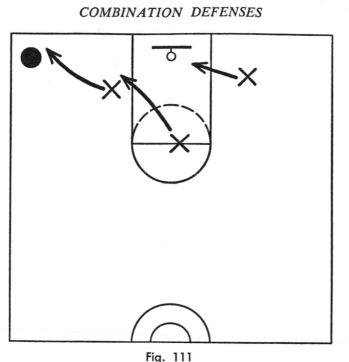

Fig. 111

ate dangerous overload situations. If they don't recognize the defense, they will be stymied, however. When they do recognize the defense, they will probably call time. That is a good opportunity for you to change you tactics or go to another defense.

The Box and One.

The *box and one* is sometimes used as a diamond and one. In either event, one man will play man-for-man while four men zone. Obviously, the one man will be assigned to guard the opponent's outstanding, super-star scoring threat. The four zone men will use the box or diamond formation from which they defend the entire critical scoring area.

The man playing man-for-man defense should strive to keep his man from receiving. The greatest value of the box

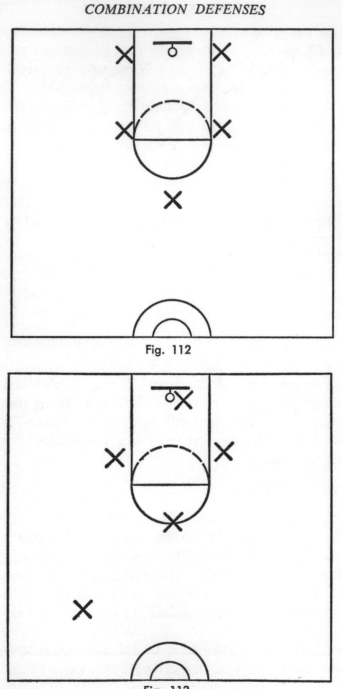

Fig. 112

Fig. 113

and one lies in its strength against teams who have concentrated a large portion of their scoring around one man. If this one man can be stymied or heavily restricted, the offense of such a team is completely demoralized. Therefore, the first objective is to keep the "hot shot," the high scorer, from receiving the ball. Of course, it will be impossible to do this 100 per cent of the time, but the fewer times he receives, the lower the score. There are other reasons for not allowing him to receive. Most super-stars are accustomed to handling the ball a great deal. When they don't get their hands on the ball often, they become nervous. This nervousness may create errors when they do receive the ball.

The most vulnerable position for attack is the middle. The four zone men should line up rather tightly on the edges of the three-second lane when the ball is at a front position (See Figs. 114, 115).

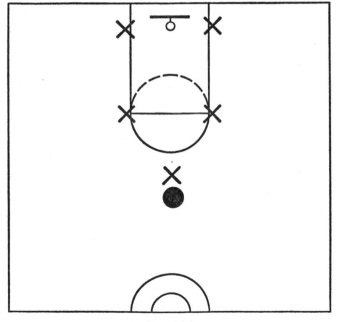

Fig. 114

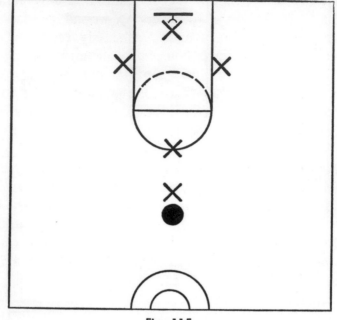

Fig. 115

If the ball moves to a wing position the zone men will take these spots. (Figures 116, 117).

A pass to the corner will be covered in this manner. (Figs. 118, 119).

There are many opportunities apparent for the offense. On a percentage basis, the four men left quasi-open will shoot more inefficiently since they are not accustomed to carrying the scoring load. The one man will shoot less efficiently since he is being "defensed" in a nerve-racking way for which he is unprepared. If the diamond zone formation is used, the slides for the various positions will be as indicated in diagrams 117 and 119.

Most offensive teams will concentrate their attack on the vulnerable middle area. They might even station their one man, who is being harassed, in the middle for the entire evening. If so, you are forced into what amounts to a 2-1-2 zone or a 1-3-1 zone.

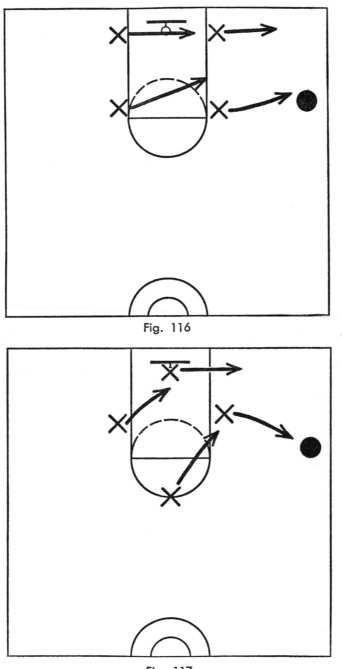

Fig. 116

Fig. 117

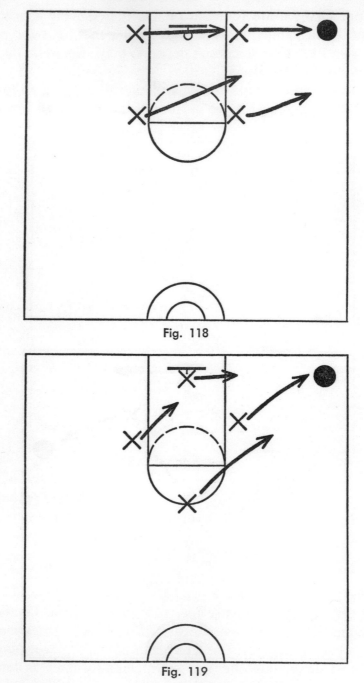

Fig. 118

Fig. 119

Your chances are four out of five that the big scoring threat is still hampered. The chances are that he is forced into a position that he doesn't desire to play. So, your plan might still be effectuated.

If the offense should use this tactic, have the man-for-man defensive player move in front of his man at all times.

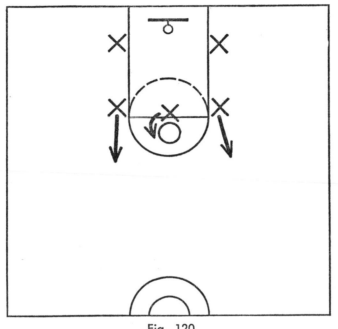

Fig. 120

The offense has served only to neutralize the vulnerable middle position and thus hamper their own scoring star. 121).

The Tandem and Three.

The *tandem and three* looks like a 1-1-3 (See Fig. 122).

It gets its name because the front two men use tandem positions (stacked) from which to defend. The three men play a base line zone. The front man on the tandem plays the most dangerous offensive guard man-for-man as long

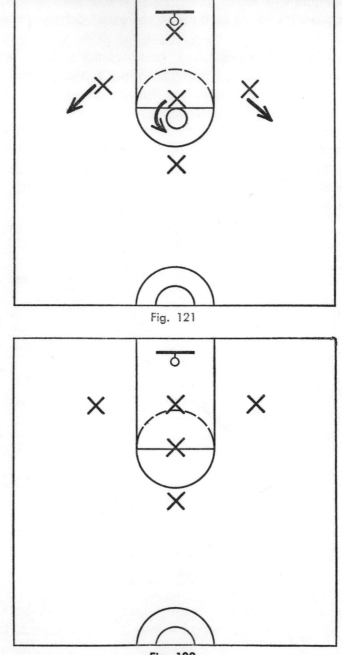

Fig. 121

Fig. 122

as that man is in either guard spot. If that man moves to a corner or out of the guard areas, the entire defense becomes zone.

This defense would work best against a team whose greatest scoring threat is an outstanding guard. Some teams have an offense that revolves entirely around one of its guards. If a team has balanced guard strength, the tandem and three would not be effective. If a team has a great guard who is the key to its entire offense, this defense would be worthwhile. That guard should receive a great deal of harassment each time he receives the ball out front. The other guard would be virtually ignored.

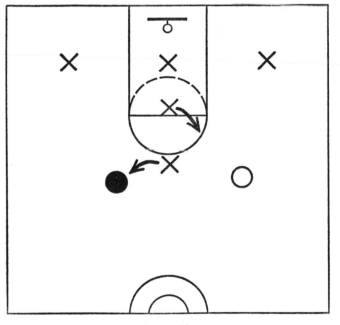

Fig. 123

The number 3 and number 4 men would play both the wing spots and the corner positions if the ball goes to those places.

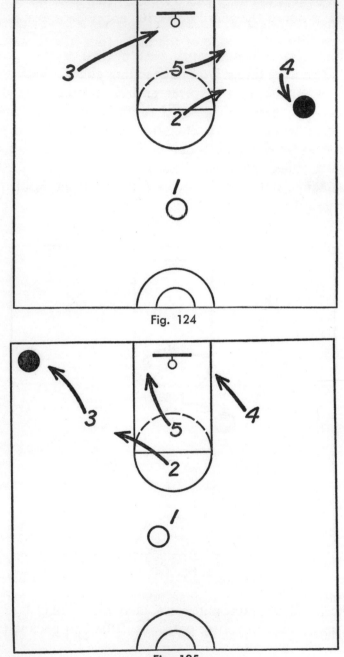

Fig. 124

Fig. 125

If the offensive guard being harassed leaves the outside area, the front man on the tandem assumes a 2-1-2 defensive slide position on the side of the ball. (See also Fig. 127).

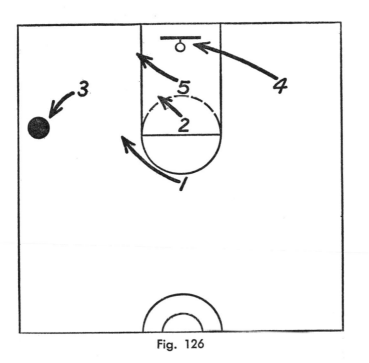

Fig. 126

The tandem and three gives the team with one big man an opportunity to keep him near the goal as in the case of number 5. He is always in good rebounding position. It would also work well against a team that does not have an outstanding pivot threat.

The Diamond Defense.

Here is a combination defense that offers good floor coverage and confusing tactics. It is not a last resort defense. Assuming you have one fast, smart defensive player and four other men willing to work, the *Diamond* can be a reliable defense for virtually any contest (See Fig. 128).

Fig. 127

Fig. 128

Numbers 1 and 5 stand side by side. Number 1 should be the best, fastest defensive player on your team; number 5 should be a good rebounder with good speed; numbers 2, 3, and 4 need have no specific qualifications other than being dedicated defensive performers.

Number 1 will cover the entire base line. If an offensive man goes into a corner or to the base line, number 1 covers him. Number 5 will fill in behind him as the second man in line with the basket. Number 1 is the quarterback. If an offensive player goes into the pivot area, he sends number 5 in that spot to play man-for man. As long as an offensive player occupies the middle area, number 5 covers him. If that area is not occupied, number 5 stays near the goal for rebounding. If the ball goes to a wing position, here are the slides.

Notice that number 1 is already moving to cover the

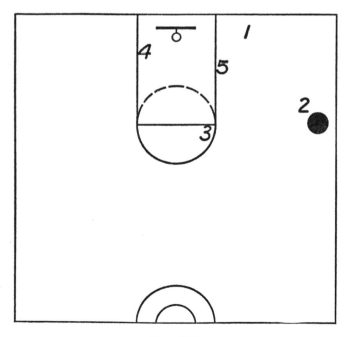

Fig. 129

corner if the ball goes there. He is in position to cover the receiver as soon as he receives.

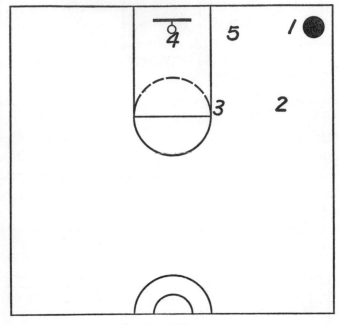

Fig. 130

These same movements (Figs. 131, 132) would be used if the ball goes into the wing or corner on the other side of the floor.

The defense looks like a 1-3-1 if there is an offensive man in the middle for number 5 to cover (See Fig. 133).

The corners are good places to double team receivers. If this method is used, the wing men, number 2 and number 4, would converge, cutting off the outlet pass and, along with number 1, create a double team. This may cause the ball handler to lob the ball out in order to get rid of it, and the point man might make an interception (Figs. 134, 135).

Combination defenses evolved from the idea of taking the best of two defenses and combining them. These de-

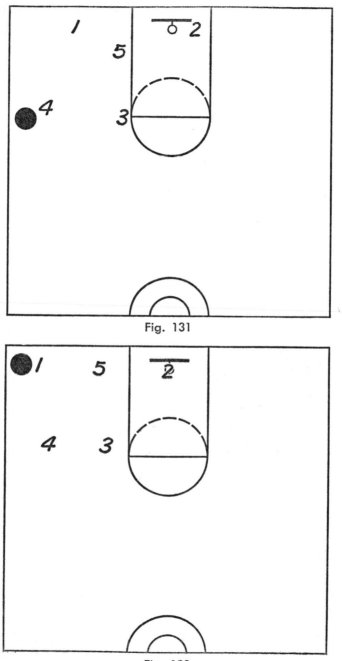

Fig. 131

Fig. 132

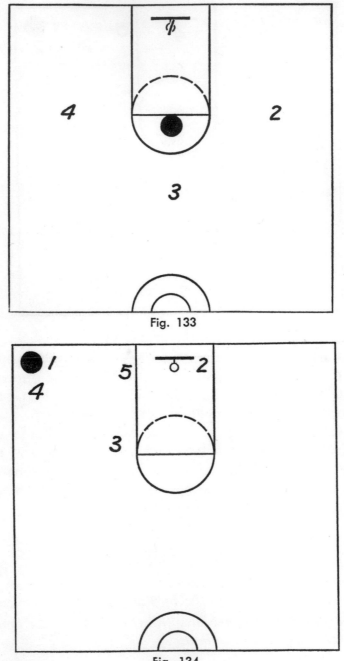

Fig. 133

Fig. 134

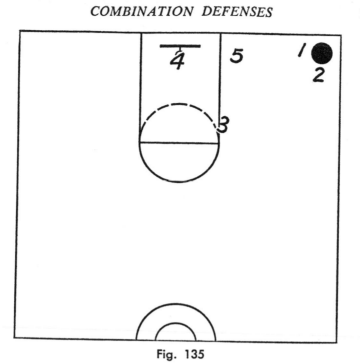

Fig. 135

fenses are unique and usually designed for a specific opponent on a particular night. The strength of the opponent determines their use. The proportion of strength at guard versus the forward strength will partially decide the use of combination. The strength of your own men will enter into the decision. These combinations are part zone and part man-for-man. They are combinations of various zone formations. The principles employed in any defense require dedicated athletes willing to take the extra step.

Teaching Hints

1. *Combination defenses are special and deserve special preparation. Be specific in your drill and instruction.*
2. *Be sure your players have full confidence in the combination defense you choose.*

3. *Use break-down drills. Take a part (two or three men) of the whole and practice it in detail.*

4. *Give your defense a chance. Don't get cold feet and quit too soon.*

5. *Prepare your combination defense several days in advance so that you will have plenty of rehearsal.*

6. *Validate your scouting information personally. If your scouting report is erroneous, a combination defense might actually help your opponent.*

9

Alternating Defenses

O NE OF THE SOUNDEST defensive innovations is alternating defenses on signal or cue. The rotation may be from zone to man-to-man or it may be from man-to-man to zone. Alternating defenses will also work using various types of man-for-man defensive play.

In recent years offensive attacks have created more and more pattern type play. These patterns or continuities employ cuts and moves that are developed into team play that is almost mechanical. They are based primarily on the assumption that the opponent will use a regular zone or a regular man-to-man defense. They are sometimes cued by the reaction of the defensive players. When these reactions are inconsistent, the offensive patterns are thrown into a state of hesitancy that breeds inefficiency. The simplest and possibly the most effective type of alternating play would result in the use of one man-for-man and one zone defense by signal. If the two formations were nearly alike in floor balance, they would be more effective. For instance, if your opponent uses a 1-3-1 offensive attack, a rotation between 1-3-1 zone and 1-3-1 man-for-man would be effective.

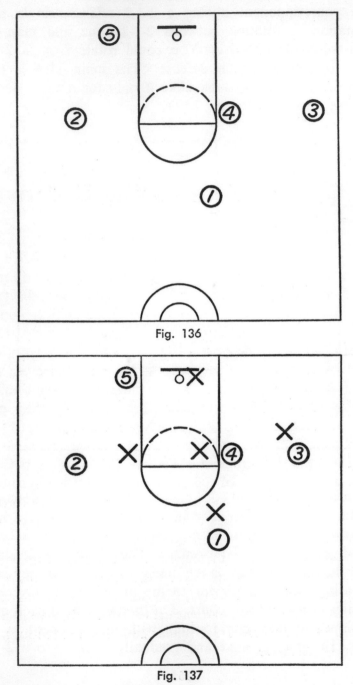

Fig. 136

Fig. 137

If your opponent utilizes a 2-1-2 offense, single post formation, a rotation between 2-1-2 zone and man-for-man would be effective. You could rotate from a 2-1-2 zone to a combination defense. The main idea is that both defenses should look alike if only for a brief period of time (See also Figure 139).

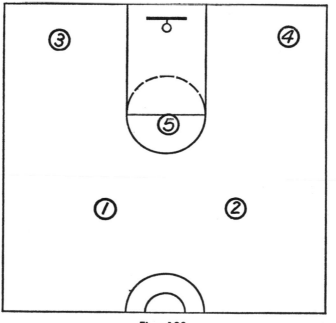

Fig. 138

Various signals and cues may be utilized. At Oglethorpe we have used a bugle system very effectively on various occasions. A basic defense is established, usually a hard-nosed, aggressive man-for-man. The players understand fully that their defense is the man-for-man unless they hear a blaring bugle note prior to the time the offensive ball handler crosses center court. On the bugle note each man continues to play man-for-man with the opponent in his area. He gives ground and gradually backs into a 2-1-2

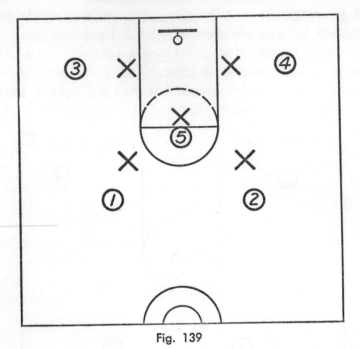

Fig. 139

zone if the opponent is using a 2-1-2 offensive formation. Each man continues to give the illusion that man-for-man defense is being played. They do this by using verbal man-for-man signals such as "switch," "keep," "play the cutter," etc. They understand fully, however, that they are to take 2-1-2 zone slides and play 2-1-2 zone defense until possession of the ball is gained.

After that particular play is completed, the entire team goes right back to man-for-man defense until they hear the bugle signal again. Obviously, the opposition is not stupid. If they were, such defensive tactics would never be required in the first place. To use such tactics is really a compliment to your opponent for this defensive maneuver will not work well against a dumb team. You must rely on the opponent's *catching on* to your tactics. When they do catch on, that is your signal to call time out and tell the players to ignore the bugle call in the future. Your opponents are now prepared to attack a zone on the bugle call.

As a coach, you should give the signal by hand movement to the bugler each time it is used. If your school has a band, the bugle system would be more subtle than otherwise. Another switch you can make when you call time out is to reverse your procedure completely. Have your team go to a zone at all times *unless they hear the bugle.* The bugle system will now be a cue for them to switch to man-for-man *for that particular play.*

Other signals and other defensive formations may be used. The score board can serve as a change signal. You might use one type of defense as long as your score is an even number on the score board, and change to a given defense when your score becomes odd. You can readily see that the only time the score can change from even to odd, or vice-versa, is after a free throw. During a free throw the ball is dead. Each player has time to collect his thoughts, prepare mentally and physically for the defensive change of plans. No words should be spoken between players since the opposition can hear, too.

Some teams have used successfully as many as four distinct defenses in alternating sequence without calling a time out and without using verbal signals. The team observed using these four defenses was a high school team. High school teams are prone to believe that this type of defensive tactic is strictly reserved for college play. The truth of the matter is that some high school teams are way ahead of the colleges in this regard.

If you prefer to use a verbal signal, here is one possibility. Let all numbers called above 20 represent a zone defense and all numbers below 20 represent man-for-man defense. Verbal signals are dangerous because crowd noises may muffle them. To lessen the danger, let a team member call the signals. The signals should be called in plenty of time for the defensive team to react before the ball crosses center line. Let your captain consistently call odd numbers above 20, indicating the zone, and even numbers below 20, indicating the man-for-man. Your opponents will decide that odd numbers represent zone defense and even numbers represent man-for-man. About the time they have your plan diagnosed, let your captain begin calling random numbers above or below the figure of 20.

If you decide to use various types of zones, a front man is the ideal one to give the signals. Since the majority of the team will line up behind him they can cue their defensive assignments by (1) his position on the floor, or (2) finger signals held behind his back. In this way you rotate from 1-2-2 to 1-3-1 to 2-1-2 to 2-3, etc. Obviously, your team must be well drilled in the use of all defenses used. It would be far better to learn two defenses well and execute these two efficiently instead of haphazard weaving of defensive formations with the resultant mass confusion.

Another way of alternating defenses is to let your offense tell you what your defenses are to be. If they have a point attack, your defense might well be of the point variety. If they have a balanced two-man front, your defense will probably be some two-man front type.

Some coaches may consider most of these plans too complicated. Winning coaches are prone to look for the sound, tried and true method that leaves no room for confusion. This policy will pay off over the long run and they know this. It is far better to have a procedure that is simple but well understood and well executed than to have one that is too complex and creates confusion in the minds of the players. However, there is no reason why these methods, with sound drilling, can't be used without creating confusion.

Here is one way to use the fairly novel and intricate idea of alternating defense without the danger of confusion. Play one defense until your opponent scores a field goal. Then change to a pre-arranged defense. This *might* mean you would not actually get into your first defense if the opponent gets the tap and goes in for the score. It *might* mean you would be in the first defense for several minutes. Challenge your team to see how long it can go without allowing the opponent to score a field goal. Once the field goal is scored, this is the cue to change to the second defense.

A free throw by the opponent may be used, but it could be tricky. If the opposition had a two-shot free throw situation, made the first and missed the second, your defense would go into its second stage unless you get the rebound. It is better to let your opponents' score indicate the change because your men have an opportunity to play out that defensive play, go down court for one offensive play, and then return to defense before changing defenses. They are able to think about the change and go smoothly into it. This procedure may be used at the beginning of any period of play. There will be no danger of missed signals. The opposition has one extra problem. They must check your defense regularly since you have proved that you will alternate. A team that sets up in one defense and stays in it all evening allows the offense the opportunity to relax. Relaxation brings better shooting. Teams that alternate will cause the offense to tighten up. The very fact that they are unsure just what the defense is going to do keeps them tense.

Some of the ideas expressed here may be more complex and extensive than you care to cope with. Still, the idea of *showing* more than one defense is excellent. If the simplest procedure is used, the danger of confusion is eliminated. The alternating idea should be used in some form. Some teams are rapidly approaching *the fulfillment* of the multipurpose defense idea. . . . a defense that flexes into several shapes and takes care of all situations. An all-purpose defense would take precedence over alternation of defenses since the former would change its appearance several times anyway.

Teaching Hints

1. *Give team members explicit reasons for alternating defenses.*
2. *Rehearse your plan so well that there is absolute confidence in it—by players and coach.*
3. *Start with a simple method before trying the more complex systems.*
4. *When possible, blend your change with the opponents' offensive formation.*
5. *Try to develop cues for changes that are subtle. Eliminate verbal signals if possible.*
6. *Don't give your opponent any worthwhile information after the game. Create more doubt in his mind if you can.*
7. *Sell your boys on the idea they are doing something that takes extra work and brain power.*

10

Concealed Defense

THERE IS NOTHING MORE EMBARRASSING to a basketball coach than to spend an entire game attacking a man-for-man defense—then learn the opponents used a zone. Those coaches who have been in the game for any length of time will probably recall just such an affair. The object of concealing the defense is to confuse the opponents so they will attack with the least appropriate offense. There are those who may think this should never happen. Possibly it shouldn't, but it has happened and it will happen even more in the future. The trends in modern basketball defense are revolutionary. The days when you can scout an opponent and prepare for one defense are over. During the heat of a contest and the bedlam of noise created in some gymnasiums, the players are often the least reliable people to determine the opponent's defense.

If the concealment works for only two or three minutes during some crucial stage of the game, it may well be enough to turn the tide. Close games have been turned into a rout in this manner.

One game was observed where the score was tied 29-29 at the half. The home team had used a man-for-man defense the entire first half. The second half they used a 2-1-2 zone with pressing tactics at mid-court and verbal

173

signals to give the illusion of man-for-man play. The opponents were confused, hesitant, and quite frustrated for about five minutes. That five minutes served its purpose. The final score was 78-50.

If you use concealing tactics and they are successful, don't let your opponent know what you used when the game is over. There is a great temptation for the coach to exhibit his sagacity. The boys are tempted to tease the opponents a bit about their inability to recognize your defense. Do a good job of conditioning your players so this won't happen. Of course, you want to be genial and visit with your opponent after the game. If you do any talking about tactics of the game just played, talk in general terms—don't give specific information. Throw up a smoke screen. If possible, confuse them even more because you will play them again that year or another year. If you concealed your defense successfully, encourage them to think they attacked your defense in the correct manner.

Here is one of the simpler ways to conceal a defense. Tell your players in the dressing room that any verbal defensive changes you make from the bench are to be ignored. At the first time out when the gymnasium is fairly quiet, yell "zone" or "man-for-man" in a loud voice. Of course, this would indicate a different defense from the one you are using. One of the opponents will be a real smart boy (if they don't have at least one smart boy, it won't work), and he will scurry around warning his teammates of your defensive change of plans. Their team will then come down the floor prepared to attack the defense you have called. If your boys do a good job of making the defense you are *actually* using look like the one you have called, the opposition will be confused for at least two or three offensive plays. Those two or three plays might make the difference.

Concealed defenses can become much more elaborate and complex. They have to become more complex in order to be effective over a sustained period of time. They take good planning and hard work. Scouting information is absolutely necessary.

One such plan is the change from one defense to another by floor position of the ball. For instance, if an opponent uses a single post offense, use a zone defense every time a pass is made to one of their forwards. Otherwise— remain in a man-to-man. This means you will be in a man-to-man defense when the ball goes to the pivot or middle area. It means you will be in man-to-man from mid-court and until a pass goes to one of the corner positions.

This defense will work best when you can be rather certain that the offense is one that concentrates on forward play. Let's take a look at such an offense.

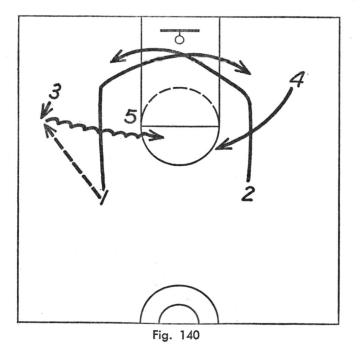

Fig. 140

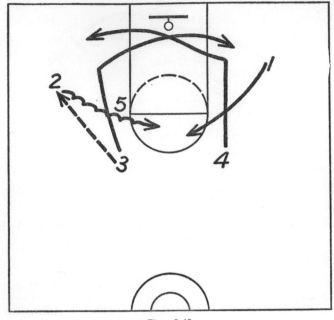

Fig. 141

Notice the continuity offered by this simple weave created by a simultaneous interchange of the guards and forwards. The receiving forward is attempting to drive off the double screen created by the pivot and the passing guard.

Your cue to change to zone defense would be receipt of the ball by the forward (See Fig. 142).

When this happens, the defensive forward should back-pedal to cover the roll-out guard. The defensive guard would play his man through to the free throw line extended and step in front of the driving forward. The defensive post man will play on the inside of the offensive post man. The weak side defensive forward should drop off to take the goal and the weak side guard will drop into the middle of the free throw line.

The first big danger is a pass to the roll-out guard.

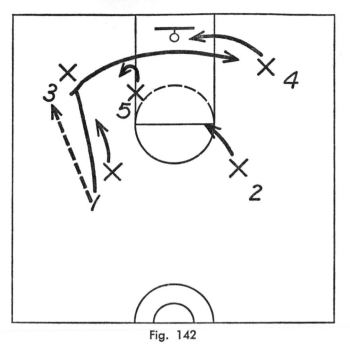

Fig. 142

Another one is a pass to the middle, although this particular offense doesn't often generate a pass to the middle from a side floor position. From this point on, the players will move in 2-1-2 zone slides. If a pass should be made to the pivot man, the defense will remain man-to-man for that entire play.

The shuffle offense has become very popular in recent years throughout the country. Patterns and tactics seem to run in cycles. A new offense or new defense appears and immediately becomes popular. After a while, the defense catches up with it and the pattern fades into obscurity to reappear twenty years later as a novel, new idea. In this case, the defense is catching up with the Drake Shuffle, one of the finest basketball patterns ever created.

Here is one way the defense has been stopping this

particular pattern. A 1-3-1 zone is actually used but concealed until the first cutter goes through to the base line.
Basic options of the shuffle are shown in Figs. 143, 144.

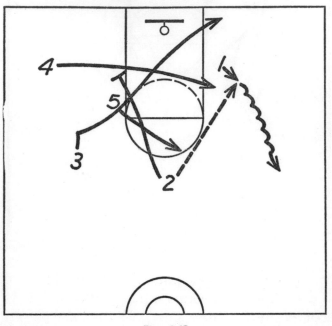

Fig. 143

Notice that 3X plays his man all the way through to
the base line just as though the defense were man-for-man.
If 2X, 4X, 5X and 1X keep their same positions, the
defensive alignment is virtually a 1-3-1 zone. From this
position, they need to take 1-3-1 slides. To use this particular defense successfully, either guard must be able to
play the base line in the 1-3-1 zone. In this particular
1-3-1 zone, the base line man will cover both corners of
the floor and the entire base line. When the ball is passed
to number 1, the low post man, the defensive guard will
trail through and take the base line and the other four
men will drop off to take 1-3-1 zone slide.

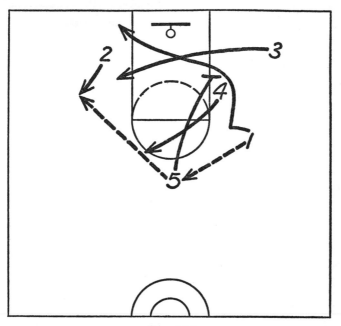

Fig. 144

The shuffle is much too versatile to defense with no more planning than this. The ball can be thrown in to the number 4 man. It can be thrown in to the number 5 man. If you wanted to be really complicated, you could let a pass to either of these men indicate a 2-1-2 zone. The simplest and possibly most effective procedure would be to use man-to-man at all times except when the ball goes to number 1.

Most shuffle teams will use a combination shuffle and static 1-3-1 formation to attack the zone when they recognize it. They will run the first cutter through and have the number 5 man step out on the weak side. The number 4 man will come into the pivot, and, while number 3 roams the base line, they move the ball around. The 1-3-1 defense would work well against this 1-3-1 attack (Fig. 145).

If this zone attack is used, your defense is already the

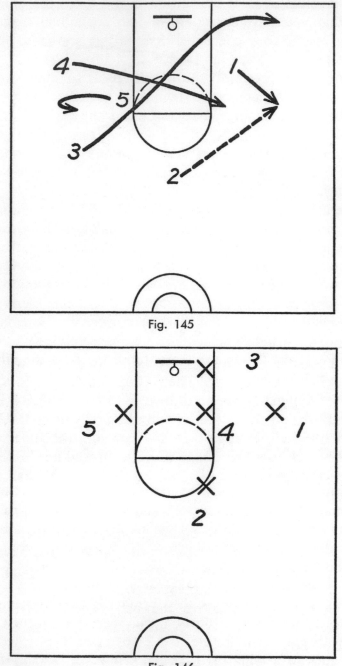

Fig. 145

Fig. 146

best possible one. If this attack is not used, the chances are that you have forced them into something new. In either event, your concealed defense has served a worthwhile purpose (See Fig. 146).

One other possibility is to shift back to man-for-man as soon as the number 5 man fails to interchange with number 2, indicating they recognize the defense. This could be too complicated and do more harm than good. Do not attempt anything that is not fully understood by the players. They must have full confidence in everything you try.

Here is another way to conceal the 2-1-2 zone against a particular type of offense. In concealing a defense it is necessary to select one that blends well with the particular offense you are to face. The 2-1-2 will naturally blend well with most single post systems. The combination *two man-for-man* and *three zone* defense would also blend well in defending against this particular offense. Here is the offense we will defend against with the concealed 2-1-2. (See Fig. 147). Notice that the initial setup for the offense puts a man in each 2-1-2 zone position.

The offense is basically a forward weave with the three front men cutting in and out of the pivot area. Against this pattern, man-for-man, a switch would occur between 2X and 4X, 5X and 3X, each time the cuts occur (Figs. 148, 149).

Your concealed 2-1-2 would work best after you use the man-to-man for at least 10 minutes. Give the offense plenty of time to fully recognize that you are using a switching man-for-man defense. The half-time would be a good time to change to a concealed 2-1-2 zone. To do this, your defensive guards should push the offensive guards a little harder as they bring the ball into play to create a man-for-man illusion. Numbers 2X and 4X are going to play their normal 2-1-2 zone positions when the ball goes to a wing or a corner. However, as this inter-

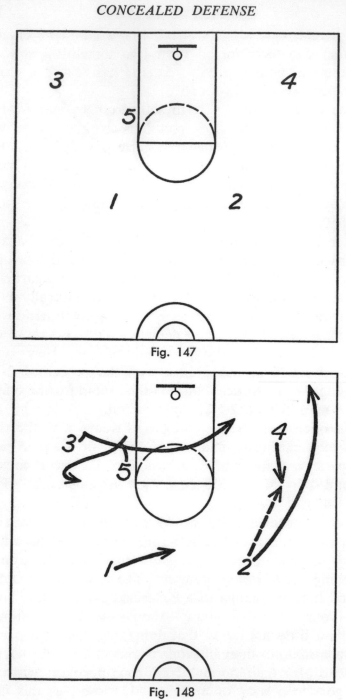

Fig. 147

Fig. 148

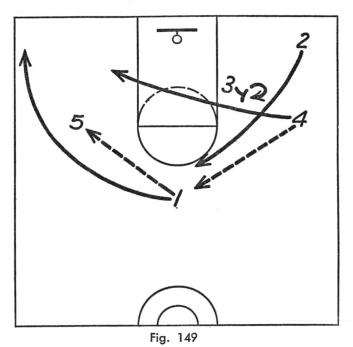

Fig. 149

change between 4 and 2 occurs, they should call "switch" in a loud voice and play the switch just as though they were in a man-for-man (Fig. 150).

Number 5X should take one step with his man when he sees him move to screen for number 3. He is actually going to play his normal 2-1-2 zone positions, but he will help the concealment if he calls "switch" and moves slightly ahead of number 3's cut to take his wing position slide. It is vital for number 3X to protect the goal when the ball is at a wing or corner on the opposite side of the floor. Fig. 151, 152 are the slides of all members with this offense having completed half its cycle.

When the ball goes back to the weak side, number 4 is going to cut off number 3; numbers 1 and 2 are going to exchange positions. Number 1X will cover the pass out to number 1 and number 3X will cover number 5 as he receives (See Figures 153, 154, 155).

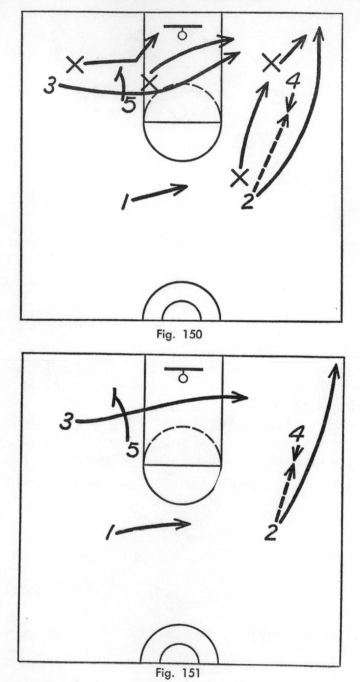

Fig. 150

Fig. 151

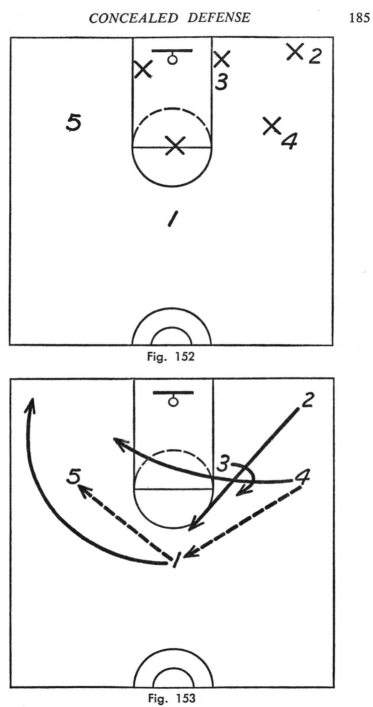

Fig. 152

Fig. 153

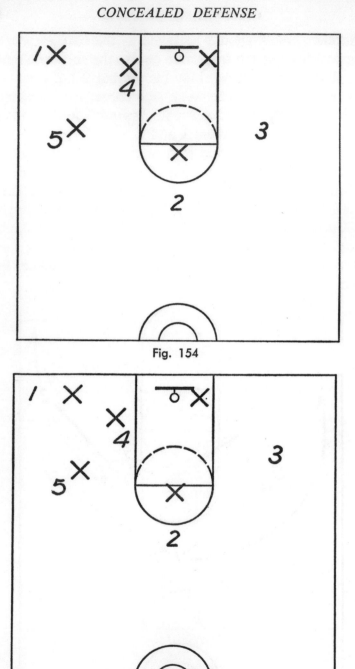

Fig. 154

Fig. 155

Another switch should be faked as the ball goes to the wing position and the front man cuts to the corner. Number 5X will call "switch" yet play his normal 2-1-2 zone positions in the middle. The weak side corner man will move to protect the basket, yet call "switch" loudly in the exchange between numbers 1 and 2.

If you will go back and look at each of these positions, the defense appears to be a man-for-man in each case with a good deal of sag on the point man. This particular pattern is very popular on the West coast. It was devised by Coach Pete Newell, one of the most astute basketball minds of all time. The offense has other options that would have to be defined and prepared for. For instance, here is one of their methods to check the defense.

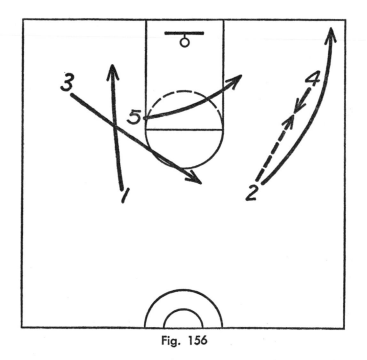

Fig. 156

You will note that there is a simultaneous exchange between players on the weak side and the strong side. The weak side men would have to fake a switch in this case along with the strong side men. Of course, the ball can go to the pivot man, and in this case you would zone. For that matter, you will be in a 2-1-2 zone at all times, but make every effort to conceal it.

One very simple way of concealing a zone defense looks like this. Set up and play a 2-3 zone defense against a single post offense.

Fig. 157

Use the 2-3 long enough for the offense to recognize the defense and initiate some sort of attack, then change your defense to a 2-1-2 zone with the front two men pressing from mid-court on back to the normal guard positions. By moving the middle man on the 2-3 higher to the 2-1-2 zone and by having the two front men harass the ball handlers, the man-for-man picture is accented.

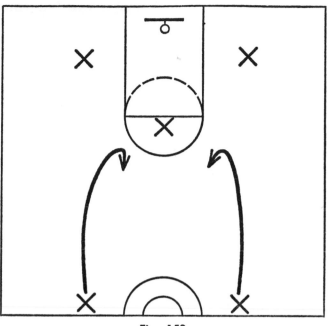

Fig. 158

Then each man in the zone should play near the nearest offensive man to further the man-for-man idea in their minds. It is vital for each man to take proper zone slides when the ball moves. It is especially important for those people responsible for protecting the middle to be alert, for some free lance single post teams will sometimes have more than one man in the pivot area.

Concealed defenses have been used at various times in the past. They have already caused many pattern or set teams moments of concern. The basic problem for the offensive teams lies in the fact that they often use completely different formations to attack a zone from that used to attack a man-for-man. The time has just about arrived when the offense cannot get away with this.

Let's assume the offense attacks a zone with a 1-3-1 static formation. This same team attacks a man-for-man with a single post two-out, two-in formation that looks like the 2-1-2 zone.

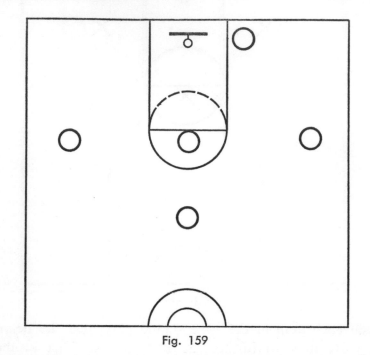

Fig. 159

Fig. 159, above, shows the zone attack formation. Fig. 160, next page, shows the man-for-man attack formation. If you are thoroughly familiar with this team and its system, you could virtually eliminate their normal offensive systems.

Set up a man-for-man and switch to the 1-3-1 zone as soon as the opponent has run one play. When they recognize, your defense and start their attack of the zone with their 1-3-1 point formation, switch back to the man-for-man. In other words, go to a man-for-man every time their offense has a one-man front. Go to the zone every time their offense has a two-man front. In this way you are "defensing" their zone attack with a man-for-man and their man-for-man attack with a zone defense. There is

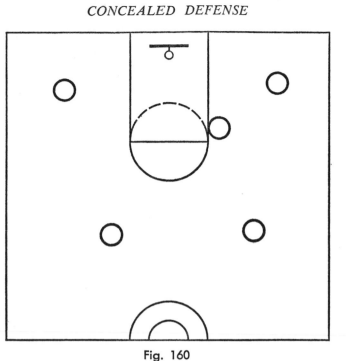

Fig. 160

little they can do about it, either. They have one alternative. They can drop both their formations and take up something they have not practiced, thus giving you the advantage.

When you scout a team and start to prepare your defense, this is one of the things you should look for. Do they use a formation that looks very similar in attacking both zones and man-for-man defense? If not, you have a good deal of leeway in preparing your defenses. If their formations are alike or look alike, the problem of concealing defenses becomes a greater one.

Teaching Hints

*1. The team with one zone and one man-for-man defense
can use concealment.*

2. *Teach well what you plan to use.*

3. *Get detailed scouting information on the opponent you plan to "defense" with concealed defense.*

4. *Let your second unit try to "defense" your first unit with concealed defenses during practice to show the value of deception.*

5. *Let opponents know that you conceal your defense, but don't let them know how.*

11

Rule Defense

THE SEARCH for an all-purpose basketball offense has been consistent since the game's inception. Each coach strives to develop a "sure-fire" method that will score under all circumstances. This glittering will-o-the-wisp has probably eluded all efforts to date. Even so, the struggle, the search and the effort have brought offensive basketball to a point far nearer its potential than defensive basketball has reached.

Defensive basketball has not received one-tenth that amount of mental and physical energy. Recent years have brought a revival of defensive basketball. It is possible this phase of the game is better than it has ever been. Coach Pete Newell and other successful defensive-minded coaches have blazed the way. They have proved that "trading baskets" is not the only way to play basketball.

Rather than relying solely on the all-purpose offense, such coaches will seek *both* the all-purpose offense and the all-purpose defense. For some it is a regular, hard-nosed, sliding, man-for-man defense. Coach Rupp's winning figure of 85 per cent over the past thirty years would seem to enhance the merits of this defense. For others the all-purpose defense is a sinking, sagging, floating man-for-man. Coach Hank Iba pioneered the principles that virtually every basketball coach uses if he sags or floats his defensive men on the side away from the ball. Some coaches have developed various types of zones to such a high degree that they simply flex or adjust to each offensive formation rather than making an over-all change.

The ideas presented in this chapter have not been fully tested. Some of the rules have been used. Other facets, such as the rule requiring each defender to follow all cutters to the key hole, have been used. The defense as an entity has not been proved under fire. We are taking the license to present this rather unique idea with the firm conviction that it is *the defense of the immediate basketball future*. We are fully convinced that *rule defense* or some closely related approach will supplant the multiple defensive formations currently in vogue. These ideas are presented in the hope that you, the coach, can use part or all of them. They are presented in the hope that they will prove to be thought-provoking. (We take this license in view of the fact that all other ideas presented in this book are tested and sound. If you have comments or suggestions concerning this chapter, they would be gratefully received by the author.)

One possibility for an all-purpose defense is "rule defense." The idea and name for this defense were borrowed from football. Football coaches have turned unashamedly to basketball for methods of training their ends and quarterbacks, so it seems fair enough for us to take an idea from them! Football teams frequently employ a system of blocking termed rule blocking. This enables the coach to give each player a few relatively simple rules with which to block for every play. It eliminates the need of teaching the blocking assignment for each individual play. If a team executes scores of running and passing plays, the amount of memorizing for each player becomes a staggering task. Rule blocking simplifies this task.

Many of us are currently using five or six basketball defenses. It seems safe to say that the team which *never* zones or *never* uses a man-for-man is helping its opponents tremendously by allowing them to specialize and concentrate on their offensive approach. Therefore, many of us are using a number of defenses to keep the opponent from getting too set in his offense. We possibly use more than one type of zone and more than one type of man-for-man or combination of the two.

Rule defense is designed to eliminate the need for teaching more than one half-court type of defense, other than pressure types. At present, it doesn't appear that rule defense can take the place of half-court pressure type defenses. Rule defense would eliminate the need for any *other* type of defense. Half and full-court presses would still have to be taught in addition to this multi-purpose defensive formation.

Rule defense should take the form of zone defense one play and the form of man-for-man defense the next. Opponents should not be able to run a disciplined offense designed to attack a zone, for rule defense will become man-for-man. They should not be able to run a disciplined pattern of man-for-man attack because it will automatically become zone in its major principles. Rule defense *should* defend automatically with the counteracting defense best equipped to stymie the offense.

Rule defense will take the shape of the offense.

If the offense is two-out and three-in, the defense should take that shape. If the offense is a single post formation, the defense should become 2-1-2 in appearance. If the offense becomes a 2-2-1, the defense should take that form. It will flex and adjust like malleable rubber to the thrust and shape of the offensive formation.

To develop rule defense, each athlete must be skilled in the use of sound man-for-man fundamentals when opponents threaten his areas of responsibility.

The half-court areas that are to be defended must be learned explicitly. These areas are shown on the chart below.

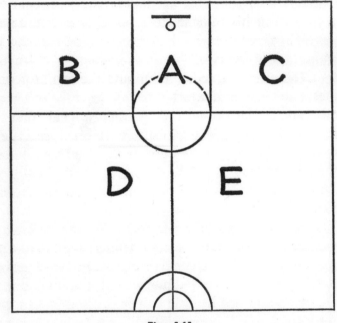

Fig. 161

Areas are designated by letters. Players may thus be designated by numerals. Only a few rules are necessary for each man to learn. The problem will be to get each man to react quickly and effectively to the many changing conditions that may occur during the heat of a ball game. The *rules* are simple. The *application* of those rules will require many hard, sweaty practice hours.

Certain words that are used in the rules need to be well defined.

Primary area—the area a player is responsible for initially. It is his primary job to protect that area.

Secondary area—the area he moves to when his primary area is not threatened. It is secondary in importance of responsibility.

One of the chief aims of rule defense is not to waste a man. With normal zones, players are often found assiduously guarding an area that needs no defense, for no opponent is in it, or near it. With rule defense, you should always have two-on-one situations and as high as four on one when the offense distributes itself in an inefficient or extravagant manner. Here are the court areas and the initial positions of the five defensive men.

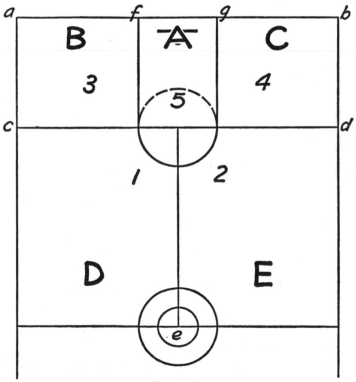

Fig. 162

Rules for each man will be different. It would seem that rules for numbers 1 and 2 should be exactly alike. This is not possible because of the necessity to defend against one-man front offensive formations.

Rules for Defender No. 1

(1) Man in primary D area with ball: guard him man-for-man (tightness dependent upon distance from basket).

(2) Man in D area without ball: sag to ball but watch D zone man closely.

(3) No opponent in D area and ball on same floor side: take secondary position where lines f and c intersect.

Coaching Pointers

(4) No opponent in D and ball opposite side of floor: take alternate position in deepest, nearest position of E area.

(5) If two men in D zone: number 1 takes the one nearest e line until he passes; then he chases the ball.

(6) Any time a single offensive man plays out front: number 1 will take him.

(7) If man number 1 is covering leaves D zone to cut for basket: guard him man-to-man until he is one full stride into A zone; return to D zone if it becomes occupied.

Rules for Defender No. 2

(1) Man in primary E zone with ball: guard him man-for-man.

(2) Man in E zone without ball: play loosely between him and ball and nearer the goal.

(3) No opponent in E and ball same side: drop off to intersection of d and e.

Coaching Pointers

(4) No opponent in E and ball opposite side of floor: take secondary position in nearest, deepest portion of D zone.

(5) Two men in E zone: take man nearest e line until or unless he passes to man nearest the side line.

(6) Any time there is an offensive one-man front and no opponent in E zone: number 2 drops off to juncture of d and g lines, takes nearest opponent.

(7) Any time a cutter leaves E zone on a cut for the goal: number 2 guards him until he is one full stride into A zone; he returns only if E zone becomes occupied.

Rules for Defender No. 3

(1) Man in primary B zone with ball: guard him.

(2) Man in B zone without ball: take position that will enable you to cover him quickly if he receives.

(3) No opponent in B zone, and none in A zone: take secondary position three feet in front of basket and help defensively with free-lance judgment play.

Coaching Pointers

(4) Two men in B zone: take the one the greatest distance from goal.

(5) Any time man number 3 is guarding leaves B zone on a cut for goal: guard him until he is one full stride into A zone and return to B area only if it becomes occupied.

Rules for Defender No. 4

(1) Man in primary C zone with ball: guard him.

(2) Man in C zone without ball: take position that will enable you to guard him quickly if he receives.

(3) No opponent in A or C zones: take secondary position three feet in front of goal and help defensivcly with free-lance judgment play.

Coaching Pointers

(4) Two men in C zone: take man deepest in corner.

(5) If an opponent leaves C area: number 4 takes him until he is one full stride into A zone and returns to his area only if it becomes occupied.

Rules for Defender No. 5

(1) Man in primary A zone with ball: guard him.

(2) Man in A zone without ball: play half a man in front of him.

(3) No opponent in A zone, take most dangerous unattended opponent in secondary area C or B on side nearest the ball.

Coaching Pointers

(4) No opponent in A zone and ball located in D or E zone: take deepest opponent in C or B areas.

(5) Two men in A zone: take man nearest the goal.

(6) No opponent in A and none unattended in B or C: play any man nearest A but be prepared to pick up cutters entering area.

(7) When any cutter moves through A zone: pick him up and keep him until he leaves it unless number 5's man has ball. Return only if the cutter voids his scoring threat by poor position.

At first glance, the rules appear to be complex and confusing. Remember that each boy has only one set to learn for all half-court defenses except presses. We are fully convinced that five, six or seven rules are easier to learn and apply than five or six different defenses with different slides for each.

Note that three of the rules apply to all players. There are extra specific, unique situations for each man to prepare himself. They are designated as *coaching pointers*. There is no need for each player to learn all of these. He need only learn those rules that apply to his area. The coach must know the coaching pointers for all areas.

Here is an example of one offensive formation and how the rules for each man will combat it.

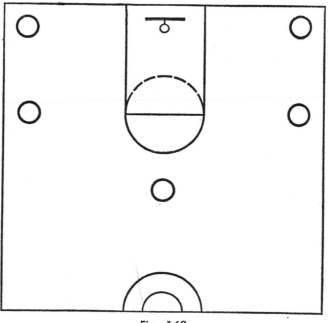

Fig. 163

The player needs to know specifically and quickly when a man is considered in his area. To help him judge, consider any man *touching* his area to be *in* it.

To cover this 1-2-2 offensive formation, each man will

simply apply the rule that fits the situation. For number 1, the sixth rule concerning a one-man front would apply. For number 2, the sixth rule would also apply. Number 3 would apply rule four. The fourth rule would apply to number 4's play here. Number 5 would use rule three when the ball goes to the B or D side of the floor and pick up the man in the left corner.

Here is what the formation and the players' actions would result in. Note that the defense has assumed a 1-2-2 formation, simply by applying the rules.

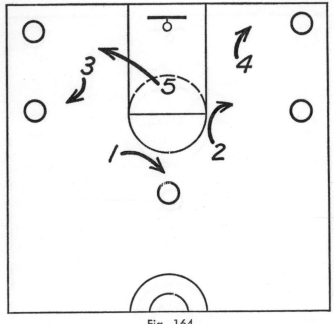

Fig. 164

If an attack is used that employs three men far out front, we will give the outside men some laxity of movement and cover all three with players 1 and 2, with primary attention given to the middle man of the three-out group. It doesn't seem necessary to cover the wide outside men, when to cover them would result in opening the middle for offensive driving.

Possibly the finest facet of this defense is its use of zone and man-for-man principles simultaneously and alternately. As a matter of fact, the opponents might well leave the game still not knowing precisely what sort of defense was used. Let's take a typical series of cuts employed by pattern type teams. The Drake Shuffle offers a fine example of a great pattern offense. Here are the basic cuts employed by the shuffle offense.

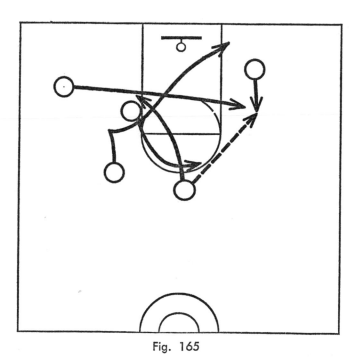

Fig. 165

Rule defense would combat this attack thus: Number 1 will defend the initial cutter until he penetrates one full stride into the A zone. There, number 5 will pick him up

and keep him all the way through the A zone. Number 1
stays where he is when number 5 takes his man. Number 5
will not return to his initial position when the second cutter
enters the A zone. Number 3 will have followed his man
into the A zone and will protect that area. Number 2
guards the passer and keeps him while he screens for the
roll-out man by applying *rule number two*. When the screen
occurs and the roll-out man comes into his area, number 2
returns by applying the clause, "return only if your zone
becomes occupied." Number 4 applies *rule one* (See Fig.
167 for player 2's action).

Fig. 166

Here are a number of formations and the shapes which
rule defense would take to combat them. Rule defense is
like a snake that regenerates destroyed tissue or like the
mythical monster that grows two heads every time one is
destroyed (See Figs. 171-176 on pages 207-209).

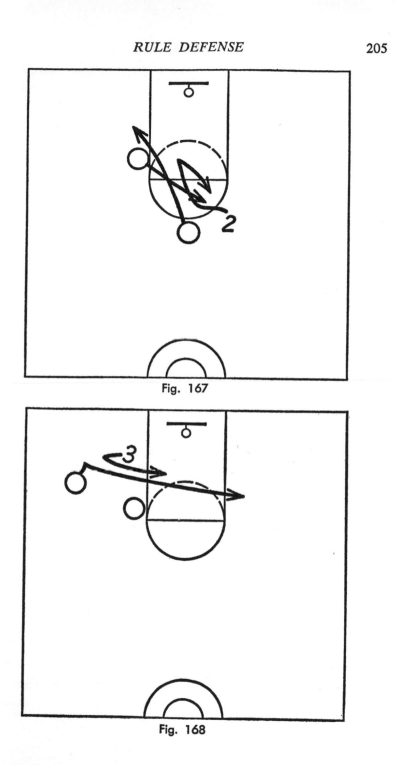

Fig. 167

Fig. 168

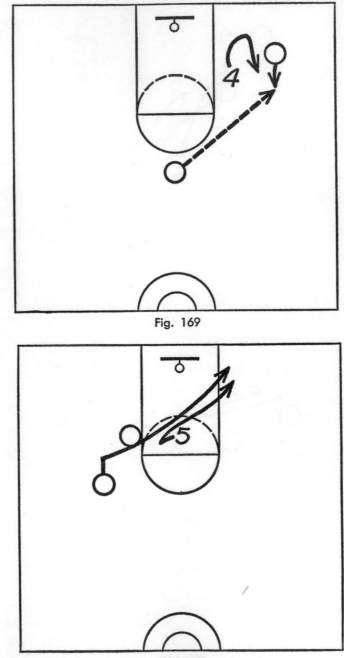

Fig. 169

Fig. 170

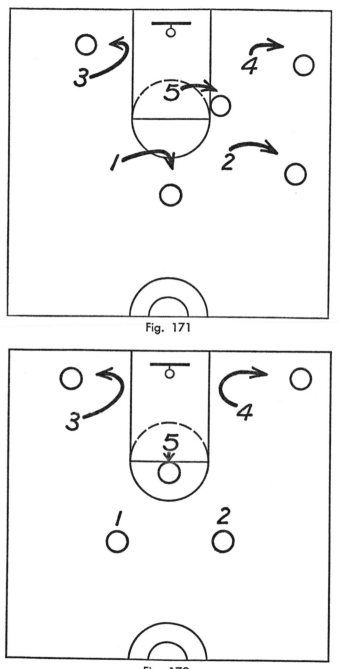

Fig. 171

Fig. 172

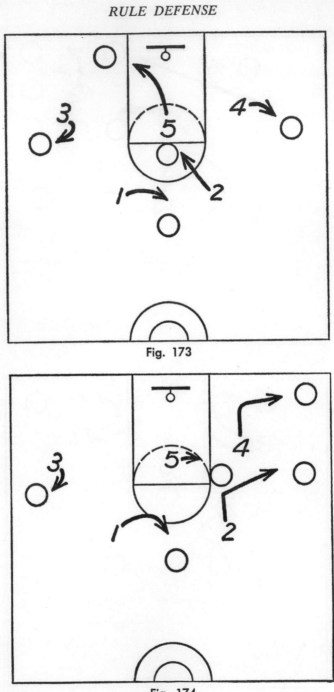

Fig. 173

Fig. 174

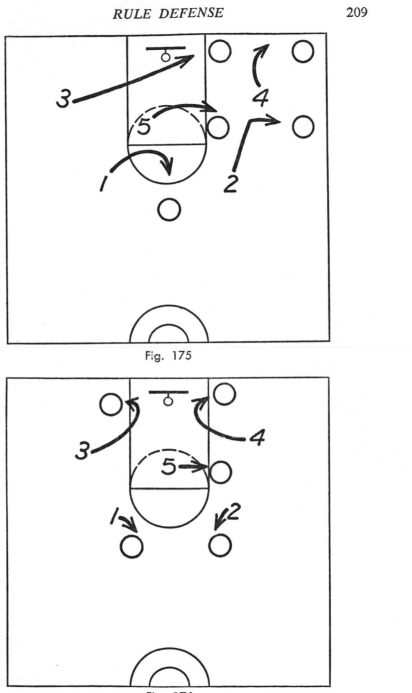

Fig. 175

Fig. 176

Teaching Hints

1. *Teach all man-for-man principles, especially one-on-one play.*

2. *Teach proper use of arms as they are employed by zone defenses.*

3. *Give each player a 3 x 5 card with his rules printed on it. Make sure that he knows each rule and further that he* UNDERSTANDS *them.*

4. *Prepare each player with a workable knowledge of every player's rules.*

5. *Give each individual a set of reaction drills each day so that his response will be automatic and quick, so that he will be* CONDITIONED *to respond to every defensive situation that could possibly be covered by use of his particular set of rules. These drills should simulate various game situations.*

6. *Give the* TEAM *reaction drills so it will be conditioned to respond as a team to game situations.*

7. *Sell them on the idea that you are doing something unique. Let them become good psychological agents by telling opponents after each game that you use straight zone, regular man-for-man, a combination defense, or other misleading information.*

12

Defensive Rebounding

THE DEVELOPMENT OF BASKETBALL, like that of most sports, has followed the line of least resistance. It is natural to develop the easy part first, then move to the more difficult. Basketball offense has received the major share of attention since the inception of the game. In recent years defense has also come into the limelight. The basketball fan is becoming aware of the contribution made by the defensive player. Sports writers are beginning to give outstanding defense the tribute it deserves.

There are three major parts to the game of basketball. Two of them have been developed to a very high degree of efficiency. The third part is a whole new frontier for exploring. It is the rebound game. Rebounding is paid a lot of lip service at various levels of play. Professional teams are especially aware of its value. Most high school and college teams keep rebound charts to determine the number of rebounds each individual gets. Still, we have not touched the vast potential of the rebound game.

If you will study films closely you will see two or three men go to the backboards. In rare cases, four men will make an effort. Even if these two, three or four men make a supreme physical effort, the rebound game at this level is similar to that of a defensive team that employs two or three men while the others take a rest. In years past, a player was considered a rebounder, a shooter, or a defensive player. We have eliminated part of this fallacious approach. The player who stands on defense straight-legged or loafs is frowned upon. Even the fans will get on his back. Yet, even now, in our modern game of basketball, we see players standing and looking, not once or twice during the game, but virtually every time the ball goes to the backboards. If these men were so indolent on offense or defense, they would be removed immediately. Why should they be allowed to remain in the game if they don't contribute to every play, offensive, defensive, and rebounding? I can see no more reason for a player standing, watching and looking on defense than for this very same thing to take place when the ball goes on the backboards. Actually, to loaf on rebound plays should bring the greater censure.

Defense and offense require speed, coordination, and other skills that rebounding does not require. Any basketball player can rebound if he has enough energy and intelligence to put on his uniform and get on the floor. He can at least block his man away from the goal and thereby fulfill his responsibility. He doesn't expect his teammates to do his job for him on offense or defense. He shouldn't expect them to carry out his duties when the ball goes on the backboards.

There was a time when offensive players were simply expected to throw the ball to a certain player and stand and watch while that one man did the entire offensive job. There was a time when certain players were not expected to rebound; they were expected simply to stand and admire while one or two *"natural born"* jumpers and rebounders went in and did their work for them. There is no place in the game for an individual who can't carry his load in all three phases of the game—offense, defense, and rebounding.

Any basketball player can become a good rebounder. A good defensive player already has a running start toward rebounding excellence. He already has courage, otherwise he wouldn't be a good defensive player. He is already accustomed to bending the legs and has developed a wide base which is excellent for rebounding. Otherwise, he wouldn't be a good defensive player. A good defensive player, no matter what his stature, should be able to carry out his rebounding duties very efficiently. Any good defensive player who isn't a good rebounder simply hasn't been given the guidance, instruction, and encouragement necessary.

The first main, obvious reason for rebounding is to eliminate the opponent's second shot. If you could play a perfect rebounding game and not give your opponent a single second attempt, you could win very easily even if they were successful on as much as 60 per cent of their shots. We are assuming that your team does its job on offense and defense. Do some quick arithmetic and figure a few percentages for yourself. If your opponents are shooting 40 per cent, and shooting seconds every time they come down the floor, what percentage of the time are they scoring and what is their real percentage? If they get the second attempt every other time they come down the floor, what is their real scoring percentage? In the first case, they are scoring 80 per cent of the time; in the second case, they are scoring 60 per cent of the time and when they get no second shots, they are scoring 40 per cent of the time. This type of figuring might explain that particular evening you lost when your team shot over 50 per cent. There are other possible factors, of course, but the number of times the second shot is gained is the most important one.

When you look at percentages in this light, actual shooting skill doesn't seem as important. Nearly all good basketball teams are going to shoot 40-50 per cent—the precise figure to be determined by the efficiency of your defense. Yet, with a simple, uncomplicated rebounding effort, your teammates can double their scoring percentages by getting the rebound and the second shot.

When viewed in this light, how can we rationalize the proportion of practice time expended on the three phases of basketball—offense, defense, and rebounding?

The proportion probably runs something like this: 70 per cent offense, 25 per cent defense, and 5 per cent rebounding. We are putting the greatest emphasis where the kids spend most of their free play hours. We are putting the least emphasis on ball possession or rebounding; yet, we speak blithely of ball possession and the blatant dangers of giving up the ball to an opponent through a violation, etc. What is the difference between double dribbling or handing the ball to an opponent and ignoring a free ball lying on the floor that could be easily possessed? Every time a basketball player fails to play basketball when the ball goes on the backboards, that is what he is doing.

Each time a basketball team goes into the offensive end of the floor, each team member has a job. Each time a basketball team goes on the defensive end of the floor, each player has a task. Each time a ball goes on the backboards, each player has a task.

If we sold this idea completely and if we could get each player to be as conscientious about performing the rebound game as well as he does the other two phases of the game, our teams would improve by almost a full third. We would jump way ahead of our opponents and, during the next decade, be considered a phenomenal basketball team. During the past ten years the team that played well on defense stayed in the limelight. The new frontier is rebounding. Those teams that exploit this fact are going to move way ahead. The time will come when this part of the game will be accepted just as we now accept defense. The time is past for shooting specialists or defensive specialists, and the time will pass when a team has only one or two rebounding specialists. We will then have a complete game and be in a position to turn our attention back to the details of fundamentals. We will be able to give more time to the all-important development of the individual physically, socially and emotionally.

In the past, we have spent considerable time teaching rebounding position, jackknife, and other techniques of the actual rebound leap. But we have been getting the cart before the horse. We have had players who could perform the break-down drill beautifully and yet fail to rebound in game situations; the very simple reason is that we were teaching the third step and putting little emphasis on the first two. The first step in defensive rebounding is the block off; the second step is moving to the board; and the third step is the rebound leap.

For offensive rebounding, this procedure would vary slightly. Movement for the goal must be made first, position gained second, and the rebound is gained third. In both cases, if we teach the first two steps well, the third step is an easy one to take. If you will study films, you will see that most rebounding is done when it is convenient, when the ball bounces right, and when a player happens to be in position. This is tantamount to guarding your man when it is convenient, or when he happens to drive in a direction in which you don't mind moving.

The Block Off

The block off is performed to secure the wide rebound. Never let a player alibi for poor rebounding effort by saying, "the ball rebounded wide and went over my head."

This player is not performing the vital first step, the block off. If you are going to give your opponent all wide rebounds, you can skip this particular teaching step. The block off should be performed as soon as the shot is taken. This holds true whether you are guarding a shooter or a man without the ball. During man-for-man defensive play, a defensive player may not be aware that the shot is up. To let him know, and to let all five men know, some team signal should be used. It is almost a waste of effort for two or three men to block off while the others allow their men to slip by to pick off an easy rebound. The block off must be performed by all five men and it must be performed aggressively. If those defensive players who see the shot go up, yell a prearranged signal, such as "shot," "rebound," "geronimo," "rack," etc., the weak side defensive players who might not have seen the shot will benefit. This is also good psychological warfare. Such a signal produces a momentary spark, a momentary team unity, a momentary feeling of *esprit* that might carry a player a little bit higher on the rebound. It also might demoralize the opponent who is faced with the fact that here is a team with all five men blocking off and fighting for the rebound. The opponent might be tempted to shoot the ball up and trot back down to the defensive end of the floor and forfeit any right they have to the ball.

The block off should be performed quickly and aggressively. Each opponent should be blocked off wherever he stands. The farther from the goal, the better. Some teams block off when the offensive rebounder gets halfway to the goal. Others allow the individual team members to block off wherever they wish. We believe the block off should occur immediately, no matter where the offensive man is standing (See Fig. 177).

Generally, this is going to create less confusion in the "snake pit" (goal area) when the actual jump is made.

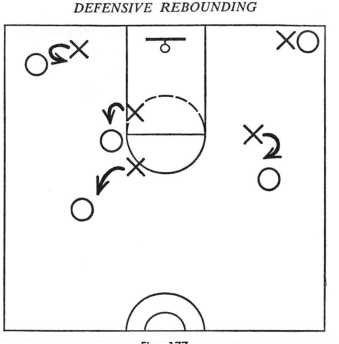

Fig. 177

Each jumper will have a maximum amount of room in which to operate. If the block off doesn't take place on the perimeter and all ten men end up under the goal, no one has a real chance to leap in an unrestricted way.

There is a rebound ring on the market that throws a wide rebound. It is shaped like a cone and looks something like this:

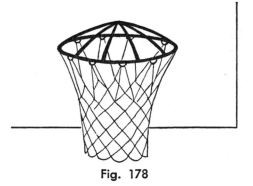

Fig. 178

This ring is designed to throw the ball wide. It might be well to attach permanently a rebound ring of this sort to one of your least used practice goals. The block-off drills on such a ring are greatly enhanced since you get a wide rebound every time. You can practice the block off on such a goal working as many as 12 men at a time. Practice the block off with no attempt to rebound. Practice the block off and retreat, leaving a big rebound cup for the ball to fall in.

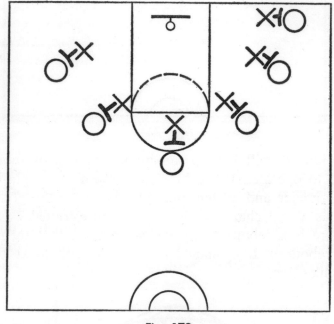

Fig. 179

Do not allow the players to jump. Fig. 180 illustrates how simple the actual rebound leap becomes if every man does his job. Practice the block off as a stationary drill in the manner we have discussed. Practice the block off with every man moving and not knowing when the shot will be taken.

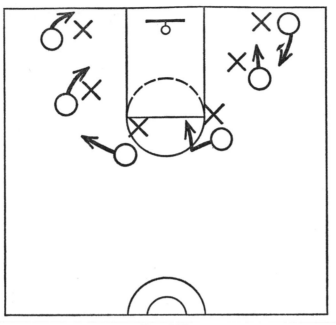

Fig. 180

Practice the block off with big men on big men, with litle men on big men, with slow men on fast men, etc. You will then indelibly impress each boy with the fact that this is one thing he can do even if he is four feet tall and guarding a man eight feet tall. The block off must be performed by everyone. A player who does not consistently perform the block off is breathing vital oxygen that should be made available to his substitute.

After the block off has been executed, the rebounder must *go to the boards*. He should release his man when the ball strikes the board or ring. He quickly determines the angle of the rebound. Then he releases his man and moves in for the rebound *whether it is convenient or not*. He goes to the boards even if teammates or opponents are in the way. Most boys become good rebounders if they take the trouble to get in contention for the rebound. They will not get in contention if they don't move on into the rebound cup area. If you will study film of basketball games, you will find very few instances of potential rebounders moving in unless they have a convenient, direct route to the goal.

As a ludicrous example, we have used a drill to prove to our men that they can reach the goal in time if they only try. We tried to show them impressively that they are out of contention only if they don't go to the boards. Players were lined up at mid-court. The ball was tossed on the boards. The players were asked not to let the ball strike the floor before they recovered the ball. Each man was surprised to find that he could do this. He realized fully how easy it would be to get to the boards with a good effort on his part from any of the closer, normal positions in the front court.

The main reason players will not go to the boards is the indirect route they must follow created by other players in the way. Because of the congestion it becomes necessary for them to change directions, stop and start, and move much as though they were running wind sprints. You should drill on going to the board just as you drill on the block off and when to release.

The first drill we have found useful involves the use of inanimate objects such as chairs. Place these chairs around the front court area at random and line your men up in three lines facing the goal but a good distance from it. Throw the ball on the boards and have your men slide through and around the chairs and reach the rebound position before the ball strikes the floor (See Fig. 181).

The next step is to use players for the rebounders to evade in their attempt to rebound. Put a group of men on the inside at various positions. Put another group on the outside. When the ball is tossed on the boards, let the outside group try to get to the boards. The group on the inside may move about but should not block off. The

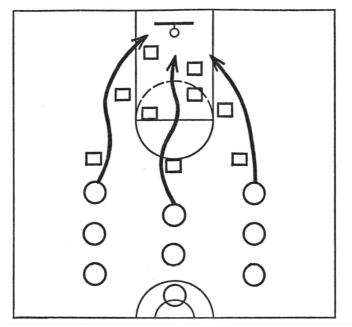

Fig. 181

outside men should not be allowed to go until the ball *strikes* the goal or boards. They should take a simulated block-off position, release and move through the congestion in time to get the ball before it hits the floor (Fig. 182).

During the course of these drills you can instill the idea of ball pursuit. The men should pursue the ball even if it does not carom directly to them. They shouldn't take the attitude that all is lost if it rebounds on the other side of the goal. Every man should pursue the ball because deflections, fumbles, or improper receiving may cause the ball to go to a man who was not actually in the ideal position to get the ball.

Some players seem to *know* where the ball is going to carom. Actually, these players do not know. They judge where the ball will go through the use of insight. By concentrating during every practice session, they learn to judge

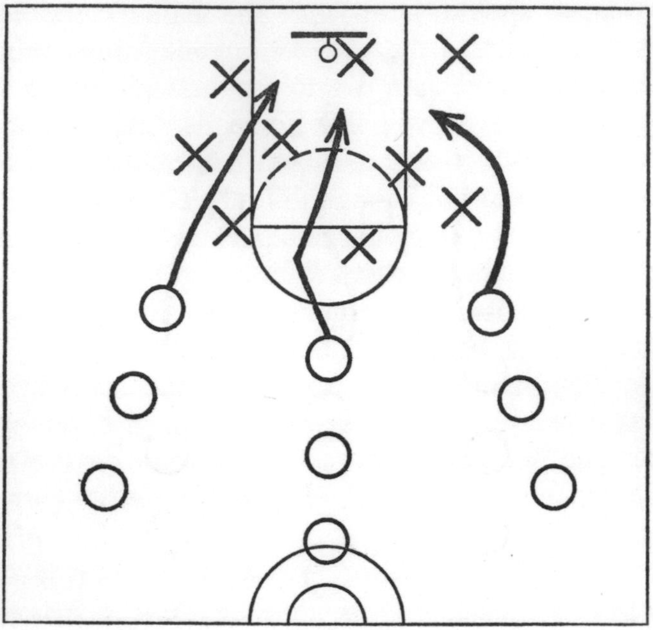

Fig. 182

where a ball will rebound according to the speed, angle, and conjunction of ball, board and ring. A player can develop this judgment if he is aware that it exists and works at it. He should try to guess every time he sees a ball strike the boards. Gradually his judgment will improve. He will be able to run around and retrieve rebounds from the opposite side of the floor. He will become that player who just seems to draw the ball like a magnet. He will become an outstanding rebounder.

Once a player has performed the block off, release, moved to the boards, determined the spot the ball will rebound to, he is still left the task of securing the ball. This is the easiest of all. It is the task we have spent the majority of our time practicing and in reality it requires the least amount of time. To secure a rebound when all teammates have blocked off well is like picking up apples that have fallen off the tree.

The leaper should jump *into* the ball. If he jumps straight up to retrieve the ball, an opponent may rebound over his back. If he jumps into the ball too much there is the chance that he will foul someone. He should *ride* into the ball about twelve to fifteen inches. Enough to insure possession and not enough to foul. The ball should be grabbed vigorously. It should be snatched with *both* hands. The rebounder should twist off the boards using a jack-knife form that insures possession. He should land in a position with legs bent and elbows wide.

To develop vigorous, aggressive rebound leaping, form two lines of players. One line should be in front of the goal and one line to the side. Toss the ball on the board and have the rebounder jump into the ball, grab vigorously, twist off and land facing the side line. The first man in the other line will jump with him and try to chop it out of his hands at the height of the jump or after he strikes the floor.

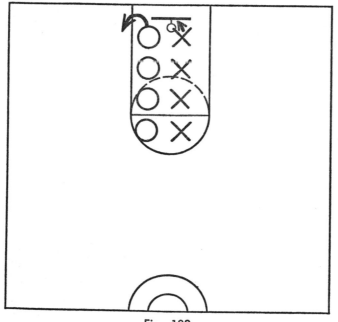

Fig. 183

Rebound charts are misleading. They tell you how many rebounds each man gained. We want the chart to tell us (1) how many times the player blocked off properly, (2) how many times he went to the boards, and (3) how many rebounds he secured. This information is sometimes very revealing. You might find that your high rebounder is getting virtually every rebound he goes after. You might find, however, that he only goes when it is convenient. It could mean that he would double his rebound output if he could only be encouraged to go every time. You might find that some unsung player is doing his job every time adequately and consistently.

Give rebound trophies on the basis of attempts versus the number gained. Do not give an attempt when the man does not go to the boards. This trophy should be an award for effort as well as for skill.

There are a number of rebound teaching aids on the market. Various companies put out rebound aids with a ball attached to a rope and spring that will cause the rebounder to grab firmly when he gets the ball. The Hickory Sporting Goods Co., of Hickory, N. C., makes a very worthwhile machine that offers a number of good drills. This machine will allow you to tip, rebound, block off, and practice going to the boards, and is adjustable to height. It causes the rebounder to time his jump and to grab the ball firmly. It is the best of the rebound teaching aids currently on the market. Inner rings that lessen the diameter of the actual goal are good for short rebounding.

Teaching Hints

1. Define the role that rebounding is to play. Be sure your boys know precisely the significance of this skill in your system.

2. *Sell the boys on the idea that they don't have to be able to be able to leap over the back board to get the ball.*

3. *Teach the team members the percentages involved in eliminating the second shot.*

4. *The block off should become second nature and as natural as the follow-through of the arm when shooting.*

5. *Use a team signal to let everyone know when the shot is taken.*

6. *Don't always drill big boys on big boys and vice-versa. Mix them up regardless of size.*

7. *Practice the block off as a static drill and also as a moving drill.*

8. *Practice rebounding without jumping at times. Make the block off so good that a leap is not necessary.*

9. *Make going to the boards a must. Make it instinctive. Make it the most important thing in life when a shot is taken.*

10. *Encourage the boys to "study" rebound angles constantly so they will be able to judge the angle of the rebound.*

11. *Use rebound teaching aids and give trophies for emphasis.*

13

Tactical Defense

Most of us have a tendency to think of tactical situations in terms of offense. The jump ball, out-of-bounds, and free throw line-ups are generally considered to be excellent scoring opportunities. Unfortunately, only one team will have an opportunity to score: the one that gets the ball. One team will be required to take the defensive. Generally each team will have the same number of scoring and defensive chances during the course of a game. It will be necessary to *"defense"* these situations just as often as we attempt to score from them. Often there is hesitation among players when these plays occur, indicating little practice time has been given to them.

A specific approach should be developed for each tactical opportunity. Although there may be many ways of "defensing" an out-of-bounds play, the fact that you have one method rehearsed and practiced gives your boys an air of confidence.

Out-of-Bounds Defense

Out-of-bounds plays run with the ball taken out directly under or near the throw-in team's goal have proved notably successful. The percentage of success on this play must be the highest of all attempted set plays in basketball. There are good reasons for this success. The throw-in team forces the defensive team to turn around and defend almost facing the goal instead of with their backs to the goal. This is strange and in itself creates lack of confidence on the part of a defensive player. The tight screen and subsequent roll to goal is possibly the toughest play in basketball to stop under normal circumstances. In this unique situation, it becomes doubly difficult. The ball handler is virtually a free passer. It is impossible to put the same amount of pressure on him that could be applied if he were in bounds where the defensive player becomes a threat to get his hands on the ball. In view of these advantages, it is not surprising that out-of-bounds plays under the goal are quite successful.

The defense must first of all realize that it is at a disadvantage, that this is a tough play to stop. The defense must make a decision to stop the lay-up or the jump shot. Surely the good, aggressive defensive team will set as its goal the defense of any attempted shot. Still, all teams would rather have the opponent take a jump shot rather than a lay-up.

One approach to "defensing" this play is a collapse to some sort of zone defense every time it occurs in a game. The zone would be used until that particular play is over. There are teams that do not use the zone in any situation so this would not be the answer for them. They would prefer using their regular man-for-man defense.

The man-for-man defense should *show* the ball handler some perimeter receivers. They should *sag* a great deal. They should sag so much that a pass to a cutter or potential scorer directly under the goal would be impossible. They should sag so much that their defense looks like a zone. The man guarding the passer should get between his man and the goal and use vigorous arm-waving tactics to prevent a direct pass to the goal area. Do not allow the offense to spread your team. Jam tightly in a knot of defensive men in the critical scoring area. If the offense spreads you they get an easy screen and roll play. If they don't spread you, they may pass directly to a receiver on the perimeter for a quick jump shot. The choice of these lesser of two evils doesn't present a difficult choice for us.

Here is the basis for nearly all out-of-bounds plays against man-for-man defenses. It may not look like this and it may be somewhat different, but the great majority of teams will use some version of the screen and roll.

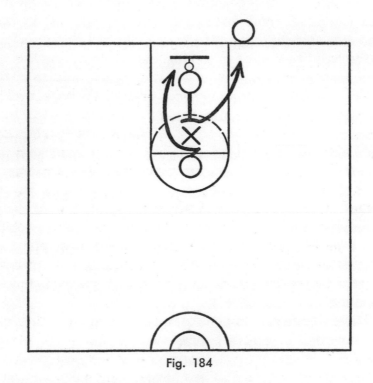

Fig. 184

If you jam this play *before* the ball is thrown in bounds, the next move is to defend against other plays when the ball is in bounds. Once the ball hits the hands of a receiver that man should receive immediate attention. Since we are sagging a great deal to make sure the middle or goal area is jammed, the receiver may be looking for the quick jump.

Our first effort is to make him hurry his shot. It is doubtful if we can stop it if the correct amount of sag is taken. We *can* make him *hurry*. If the rush to defend the receiver is too quick, we are vulnerable to the fake and drive.

Until the ball is thrown in bounds, all man-for-man defense should be *non-switching*. A deep sag is used to jam the middle. Sliding is much easier to execute from a sagging defense. The switch is capitalized on by most teams in setting up their out-of-bounds plays. They rely on the fact that you must switch and usually look for the roll-off man who sets a screen forcing the switch. Do not switch as long as the ball is out-of-bounds. The danger of having the roll man beat his man to the goal is multiplied because of the angles created by the ball being behind the boards. The problem is completely different from that presented by a switch situation when the ball is out front. Slide on all cuts. Slide until the ball is thrown in bounds. Then use whatever you normally use. If you are a sliding team, continue to slide. If you are a switching team, revert to your switching tactics. Once the ball is in bounds and normal defensive play is in progress, all actions become just as if the opponent had brought the ball down the floor for a regular play. As long as the ball is out-of-bounds in the hands of an unrestricted passer, there is nothing normal about the defensive situation.

Defensive men should take a position so that they can see potential screeners behind them. This is not always possible. If they take a quick look at the ball when the referee hands the ball to the passer, they need not worry about ball position since that man cannot move after the official gives it to him. The primary vision should be applied to one's own man. The secondary vision should be utilized to spot potential screeners. One of the hands should be behind to feel for screeners. Each team member should be a committee of one to spot and warn teammates of screeners. Defense of this difficult situation requires the highest degree of team work. In nearly every case, one of the in-bounds men is going to get screened before the ball is thrown in bounds. In some cases, more than one screen will be set. Each man should be alert to warn the men being screened. The men being screened should have a deep sag and be feeling for the screeners. Every out-of-bounds defensive play should be a challenge. Every time the defensive team stops it they should feel a glow of team pride. Every time they can make this difficult play they should develop more confidence. Team unity should be just a little bit better, for real team work is required to handle this assignment.

Here is another possible approach to defending against out-of-bounds plays. Let the player guarding the throw-in man drop off and stand directly under the goal to insure the fact that no lay-ups will be gained. As soon as the ball is thrown in bounds, he should recover to a normal position on his man.

Side line out-of-bounds defense presents an altogether different challenge. The offense should be pushed hard to get the ball in bounds. The man guarding the passer or out-of-bounds man should sag. Most side line plays will result in the throw-in getting the shot. Here is a typical out-of-bounds play from the side line throw-in (Fig. 185).

If the man guarding the passer pushes too hard, he might get screened and be unable to recover in time.

All defensive men guarding potential receivers should overplay their men. Give the opposition no free throw-ins from the side line position. Most offensive teams prepare for just such a situation. Most of them will bring their center up to receive the throw-in since they feel that the average defensive post man will not be as fast as other defensive men.

If you can push receivers hard, it causes the man throw-

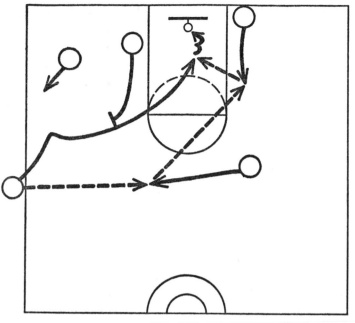

Fig. 185

ing the ball in bounds to get nervous. He might lob one or throw a slow pass that can be intercepted. He might throw it away completely.

There is not the danger involved with out-of-bounds plays under the goal. All defensive men are able to play in their regular back-to-the-goal positions. The ball is thrown from the front much as if the opposition were bringing it down court for a normal play. The biggest danger is to the man guarding the passer.

Jump-Ball Defense

It is to be hoped that jump-ball defense will become less of a problem in the future. It is certainly to be desired, for this is a part of basketball that holds little appeal for the fans. Still, jump-ball situations will occur several times each game, usually from 10 to 15 times. The jump ball occurs at center line, on the offensive end of the court and on the defensive end of the court. Actually, there are many times the jump ball may be considered an offensive play, no matter where it occurs. There are times when it will be considered defensive no matter where it happens. Whether it be offense or defense depends on who is jumping.

We will look at the jump-ball setup from the defensive standpoint only.

The center court jump is traditionally "defensed" with the tandem formation. This is the ultimate in conservative play. Even so, it is good defense for that particular play. The tandem requires two men to drop back and play in such a way that they can stop a quick tap and fast-break play from achieving a lay-up. This is basically a lay-up defense. It offers some hope of interception by the other men playing on the center circle perimeter, but the real value of the tandem is in stopping the lay-up.

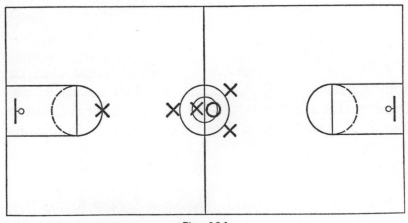

Fig. 186

This formation can be adjusted to varying degrees of conservatism. The tandem can be deep or fairly close to the center court circle. The amount of caution depends on the situation.

Another good defense that is cautious but almost sure to prevent a quick basket requires every defensive man to get between his man and the opponent's goal. This assures the opposition ball possession, but there is always the possibility that the tapper won't take advantage of the sure back tap between his men. In this case, the defense has a very good chance for interception.

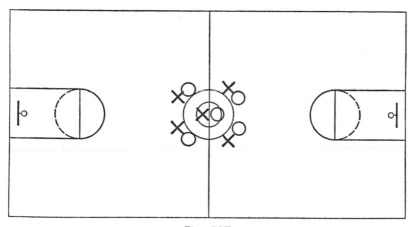

Fig. 187

Here is a system that combines some of the ideas of both systems already described. It offers concealed defense in that the defense doesn't develop until the ball is tossed. It is not quite as sure since movement is involved and an attempt at intercepting is made. It is more daring and offers the possibility of ball possession without a great deal of danger being involved.

When the ball is tossed, number 2 breaks to the free throw line of the opposition for safety's sake, in case the gamble doesn't result in an interception. This gives you assurance that the offense will not get a lay-up. Numbers 1, 3 and 4 move as indicated.

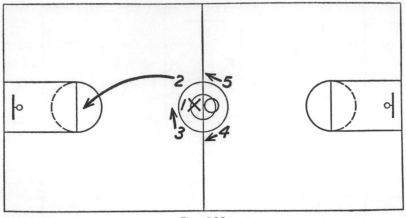

Fig. 188

This is the sort of play that might well be utilized by short teams when they are fairly sure they won't get many center lineup taps during the normal jump situation.

Jump-ball defense at the opponent's goal is the most dangerous. Proximity to the goal gives them added incentive to receive well. Do not give them an opening to the goal after they receive. Do not gamble in this jump-ball circle. Line up inside out or with one man in between every offensive pair. This assures them the ball, but closes all gates to the goal after they receive (Figs. 189, 190).

When jump-ball situations occur under your own goal, the opposition is 73 feet from its own goal. This means you can gamble here more than in any other jumping circle. You have time to recover before the opposition can score, if you prepare for that eventuality.

One of the oldest and best ways to play this is to have each man line up with his own man. Let the offense believe it is going to get a sure tap. Once the ball is touched by a jumper, let every defensive man attempt the interception. Try this as a five-on-five drill and you will be amazed at how many times the defensive team or the one with the shortest jumper will come up with the ball.

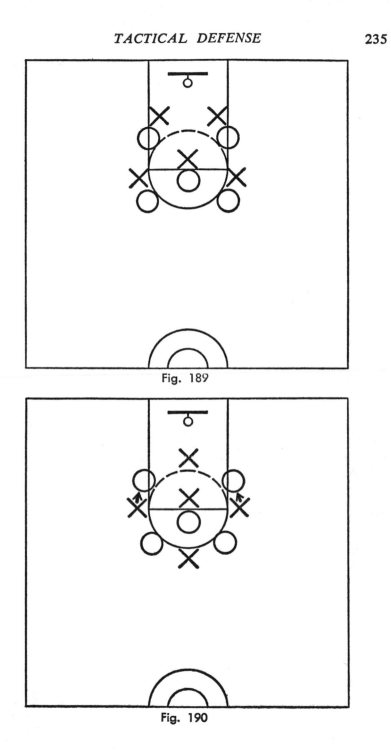

Fig. 189

Fig. 190

Another way is to use the rotation to a tandem after after the ball is tossed. Here is one more rotation system that is a calculated risk. It leaves one man completely free. In this case it is the right rear man. We will assume in this case that a right hander is jumping and tapping with his rght hand. The best man to leave open is number 3. The tapper would have an awkward move to make if he successfully tapped to that man. We will put one and one-quarter men on every other potential receiver. This offers pretty good chances of interception and gives us good defensive alignment to stop the fast break if our gamble doesn't work for an interception (See also Fig. 192).

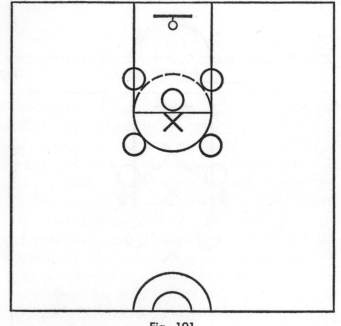

Fig. 191

Free-Throw Formation Defense

Preparing for this situation involves only two possible plays. The opponent shoots or your team shoots. The

Fig. 192

first thought is to stop the fast break when your team shoots, if the shot is missed and ball possession is lost. To accomplish this, follow one simple rule. Match the opponent in manpower. Some teams will line up in some very unusual formations to try for the fast break. You must match them in manpower and floor position. If they put two men down court for the possible long pass, you must put two men down court with them. If they put two men back on either side of the key hole for possible tap outs, you must put two men there to cover them. The guiding rule is to match them. Here are some situations that you may have to match at some time (See pp. 238, 239).

When the opponent shoots, you can play one of two ways. You can play for the fast break or you can play for ball possession. We will concern ourselves with the defensive play of this situation.

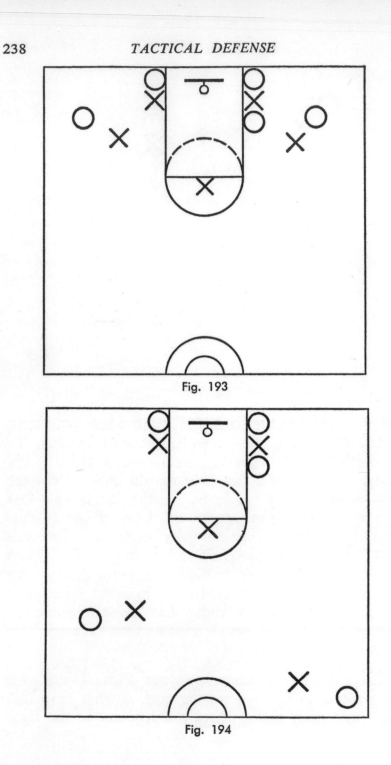

Fig. 193

Fig. 194

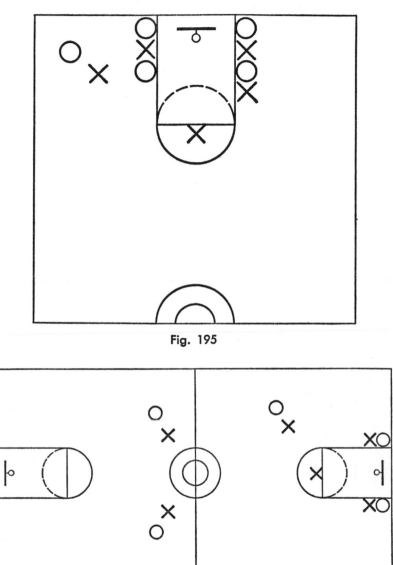

Fig. 195

Fig. 196

The strongest rebounder on your team always takes the position to the right of the goal. Studies have indicated that most missed shots will rebound to the right.

Therefore, it seems to be the best place for the strongest rebounder. Most teams will try to tap the ball back to the shooter if the shot is missed unless ideal tipping position can be gained. Since you have two men under the goal, it will be difficult for the opponent to get ideal tipping position. They will probably tip back to their shooter in most cases. The shooter should be covered by two men. One should move in front and one should move behind him.

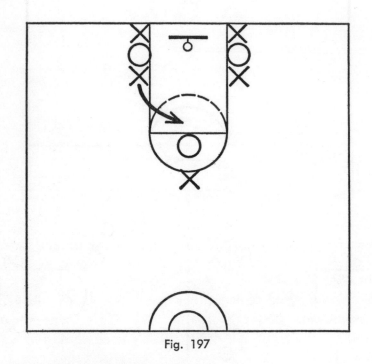

Fig. 197

The other deep man underneath must buff out and make sure that the man on his right does not get the ball. The new floor marking creating a 12-inch neutral zone makes this task a bit easier. The number 4 man can play in one of two ways. He may move straight into the front of the rim around the defensive man on his right. This move would pinch the defensive man tightly and almost insures that he will not get the ball.

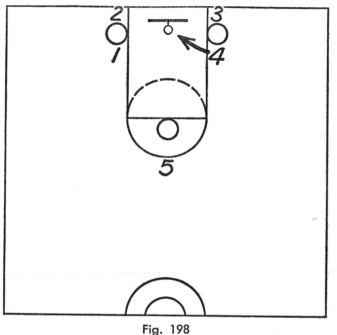

Fig. 198

Or, he can run around the defensive man and cover the small area immediately to the side of the goal on the right (See Fig. 199, next page).

We recommend that number 4 mix his moves and keep the opposition guessing on this play. This tactic is employed on the right side since most missed shots rebound that way.

Teaching Hints

1. *Be specific in your explanation of tactical defense.*
2. *Select one approach and make your players believe it is best.*

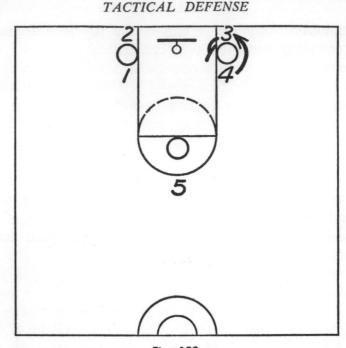

Fig. 199

3. *Time spent on defending against the out-of-bounds situation under the goal is well spent.*

4. *Sell your players on the idea that all is not lost if your opponent is taller in the jump-ball situation.*

5. *When your team shoots a free throw, always match your opponent in man-for-man strength and floor balance.*

6. *When your opponent shoots, be sure the shooter is covever and your best rebounder is lined up to the right of the goal.*

Conclusion

Defensive excellence is more than efficient execution of fundamental defensive skills. Some players achieve a yeoman's degree of efficiency and consider that adequate. The yeoman's approach is adequate, but is far from being the championship approach. The "I did my job" approach will not bring home the big trophies.

Before defensive excellence can be achieved, each player must get a really solid thrill out of performing his individual defensive skills within the framework of the team defense. He must be lifted by a great play performed by a teammate. He must be quick to commend teammates for good defensive application.

Duty defense is often performed by the outstanding offensive player who knows he must do the yeoman's job in order to play. Duty defense or the "I've got to do it" attitude will not bring the spirited play in the clutch that is the trade mark of the champion.

The first and most important task of the coach who wants defensive spirit and pride among his team members is the selling of defense to each individual and to the whole group. First, you will get lip service to defense. If you give a trophy for the best defensive player you will get a spirited performance by those boys who don't have much of a chance to win the offensive trophies. If you keep team defensive statistics, newspace engendered by outstanding defensive performances will help a great deal. If you can hold a fine team to a low team point total, it will cause team defensive pride to begin to take shape. Selling defense takes time. Once accomplished, it will literally carry itself after that. Each successive squad of men will strive to out-perform the preceding team. A defensive tradition will have been set that cannot be broken. A winning spirit will have been defined. An outspoken disgust for lazy performances by anyone (teammate or opponent) will become evident among your team.

Let each player rate himself defensively before the season starts. While each player is rating himself, the coach should be rating the entire team. Compare the results and discuss the status of each boy with the individual team members in private conversation. Use some sort of guide in making your ratings.

1. The *novice* defensive player is probably striving to "defense" the man with the ball. However, if that's *all* he can do he is still a novice.

2. The *intermediate* defensive man can defend against his man—with the ball and without the ball. He can handle his man in any situation, whether he has ball possession or not.

3. The *good* defensive player can also handle his man with or without the ball and switch or slide properly. He can switch if that is the system the coach uses. He can slide if that is the system the coach uses. He can switch *and* slide if that is the system being taught. He can do these things as well as defend against his individual opponent with or without ball posession.

4. The *great* defensive player can guard his man with or without the ball. He can switch or slide, according to the system used. In addition to these skills, he knows when to double team; when to help with the pivot man; when to talk and pep up the team, and when to push the dribbler out front. In short, he is the epitome of defensive excellence. He is the man you assign to the opposing "hot shot." Just because you assign a man to the opposing "hot shot" does not make him a great defensive player. Few teams have one. Most teams do not have all five men as high as the novice category. Few have intermediate defensive players and only rarely do we find a good defensive man. A team that has one great defensive man is fortunate indeed.

Challenge each man to move up one notch during the course of a season. Give verbal plaudits for good defensive play in practice and in games. Seek press notice for outstanding defensive play.

Most observers will say that the soundly drilled defensive team is a well coached team. I shall not argue with them. Surely it is easier to sell offensive play to basketball players. Surely defensive excellence is achieved only after much thought, work and salesmanship. Display your coaching excellence by displaying a fine defensive basketball team. It cannot be done in the dressing room at half time. It cannot be done by giving 10 minutes a day to defensive drills. It cannot be done by pre-game oratory. It must be done in detailed day-to-day practice of fundamentals.

Be sure your team is knowledgeable concerning defense. How many players have ever tried to define the defensive fundamentals? They all know the *offensive* fundamentals. If you don't like the categories we have used in this book, define your own and make sure your players know them. When you run a drill, make sure they know which fundamental you are practicing.

Take pride in the basketball skills requiring courage, stamina, persistence and character. They are defense and rebounding. Sell the game of basketball at its best. At its best, it is not a sissy sport. Put these skills constantly before the public and basketball esteem will rise.

Develop outstanding defense and you will get the finest coaching thrill of your career. There is no sense of achievement quite like it. You can originate a basketball offense. You can become "Coach of the Year" for your region every year. Still, there is no thrill compared with the one you will experience when your boys play an inspired, courageous defensive game to win the one they were *not supposed* to win.

Index

INDEX

A

Aggressiveness, 3, 216
Aids, rebound teaching, 224
Alternating defenses, 165-172
  in rule defense, 203-209
Arm movement, 19, 57, 67, 227

B

Ball handler:
  guarding, 19-20
  harassing, 57
Ball pursuit, 221-222
Base line drive, 21
Blocking, rule, 194-195
Block off, 215-219
Block out, 30-32
Body checking, 38-39
Box and One defense, 147-153
Breaks, 18, 36
Bugle signals, 167-169

C

Chair drills, 220
Charts, rebound, 224
Coaching:
  alternating defenses, 169-170,
    172
  block out, 31
  combined defense, 141-142, 163-
    164
  concealed defense, 191-192
  fundamentals, 18-32

Coaching: (*cont.*)
  importance of, 16, 32, 243-244
  leaping, 223
  matching zone defense, 120
  pressure zone defense, 122, 136-
    138
  rebounding, 215, 218-221, 225
  rule defense, 195, 198-200, 210
  signals, 169
  tactical defense, 241-242
  zone defense, 110-112
Combination defenses:
  box and one, 147-153
  coaching, 141-142, 163-164
  diamond, 157-160
  tandem and three, 153-157
  triangle and two, 142-146
  using, 141-142, 161-163
Concealed defense, 173-192
  in rule defense, 203-209
Confidence, 7, 11, 227
Confusion, 55, 113, 125, 151, 174
Court areas, 197
Cushioning, 40
Cutters, guarding, 23-24, 43-44

D

Defense:
  alternating, 165-172, 203-209
  concealed, 173-192, 203-209
  duty, 243
  free-throw formation, 236-241
  jump-ball, 231-236
  make-believe, 8-9

Defense: (*cont.*)
  matching zone, 113-120
  out-of-bounds, 226-231
  pressure zone, 121-138
  role of, 7, 11, 193-194
    increasing, 12, 171-172, 211
  rule, 194-210
  stunting, 140
  zone, 77-79
  1-2-2, 89-94
  1-3-1, 99-110
  2-1-2, 79-89
  3-2, 94-99
Defensive play:
  attitude, 3-16, 226, 242-243
  combinations, 141-142
    box and one, 147-153
    diamond, 157-160
    tandem and three, 153-157
    triangle and two, 142-146
  fundamentals, 18-32, 192-194
  man-for-man:
    pressure, **36-54**
    sinking, **55-74**
  rebounding, 212-225
  tactical situations, 226-242
Dehnert, Dutch, 23
Diamond defense, 157-160
Diamond and One defense (*see* Box
    and One defense)
Double team, 27, 47-49, 125-126
Drake Shuffle, 68-74, 177, 203
Dribblers, guarding, 20-22, 40-41
Drills:
  alternating defense, 170
  and coaching, 244-245
  block off, 218
  break-down, 164
  chair, 220
  defensive break, 18
  getting to the boards, 220
  jump-ball, 234
  pressing, 125
  quarter eagle, 7

Drills: (*cont.*)
  reaction, 210
  rebound, 218-223
  signal, 169-170
  spot, 109-110
  zone defense, 110
Duty defense, 243

F

Faking, 19, 46, 174
Fast-breaks, 36, 78, 94
Films, studying, 211-212, 215, 220
Floor marking, 240-241
Football methods, 194-195
Formations, combatting offensive,
    204-209
Fouls, 126
Free-throw formation defense, 236-
    241

G

Guarding, fundamentals of, 19-26
Guards, outstanding, 155

H

Hickory Sporting Goods Co., 224
High school teams, 7, 169, 211

I

Iba, Hank, 5, 55, 194

J

Jackknife, 223
Jump-ball defense, 231-236

L

Leap, rebound, 223-224
Loafing, 74, 212
Lob pass, 62-63

M

McLendon, John, 4
Man-for-man defense:
 pressure, 36-54
 sinking, 55-74
Matching zone defense, 113-120
Morale, team, 13

N

Newell, Pete, 187, 193

O

One-three-one zone defense, 99-105
 player assignments, 106-110
 matching, 114-116
One-two-two zone defense, 89-94
One-two-two zone press:
 full court, 128-132
 half court, 133-136
Out-of-bounds defense, 226-231
Overplay, 37-38, 42

P

Pendulum pressure, 50-54
Pivot criss-cross, 23-24
Player assignments:
 against shuffle offense, 178-179
 combined defense, 142-164
 concealed defense, 176-192
 matching zone defense, 113-120
 pressure zone defense, 121-138
 sinking man-for-man, 58-62
 zone defense:
  1-2-2, 89-94
  1-3-1, 106-110
  2-1-2, 78-89
  3-2, 94-99
Players, basketball:
 physical qualities, 15, 212-213
 star, 9-10, 149, 155, 214-215, 243
 versatility, 25, 35, 244

Practising, 213-214, 226, 245
Pressure zone defense:
 advantages, 121-123
 coaching, 122, 136-138
 one-two-two, 128-136
 when to use, 123-126
Primary area, 197

Q

Quarter eagle, 7-8, 19

R

Rebounding:
 aids, 224
 and defense, 5-6
 and sinking, 56-57
 block off, 215-219
 block out, 30-32
 coaching, 215, 218-221, 225
 importance of, 213-214
 leap, 223-224
 moving to the board, 219-222
 player qualities, 212-213
Referees, utilizing, 125-126
Ring, rebound, 217
Rule blocking, 194-195
Rule defense:
 coaching, 195, 198-200, 210
 explained, 195
 half-court areas, 196-197
 need for, 192-194
 player assignments, 198-204
 using, 204-209
Rupp, Adolph, 5, 29, 193-194

S

Scoreboard signaling, 169
Secondary area, 197
Shuffle offense, 177-179
 Drake, 68-74, 203
Signals:
 alternating defense, 165

Signals: (*cont.*)
  bugle, 167-169
  calling, 27
  novel, 171
  psychological, 216
  scoreboard, 169
  surprise, 124
  verbal, 46, 169-170
Sinking man-for-man, 55-57, 62-74
  player assignments, 58-61
Sliding, 29-30, 117
"Snake pit," 216
Sports writers, 211
Stance, 18
  comfortable, 7-8
  defensive, 22
  quarter eagle, 7-8, 19
Star players, 9-10, 149, 155, 214-
    215, 243
Stunting defense, 141
Switching, 26-29
  non-switching, 229

T

Tactical defense:
  coaching, 241-242
  free-throw formation, 236-241

Tactical defense: (*cont.*)
  jump-ball, 231-236
  out-of-bounds, 226-231
Tandem and Three defense, 153-157
  in jump-ball defense, 231-232
Teaching (*see* Coaching)
Three-two zone defense, 94-99
Triangle and Two defense, 142-146
Trophies, 224, 243
Two-one-two zone defense, 77-79
  concealed, 181-187
  matching, 116-117
  player assignments, 79-89

V

Verbal signals, 46, 169-170
Versatility, 6-7, 25, 35, 244

Z

Zone defense:
  1-2-2, 89-94
    pressure, 128-136
  1-3-1, 99-110
  2-1-2, 79-89
  3-2, 94-99
  matching, 113-120
  pressure, 121-138
  using, 77-79